The Adventures of Kilimanjaro

And African Safari

- Vikas Pawar -

ISBN: 979-8-66-908284-0

Dedicated To:

Aai and Dada

Beloved Parents, Guiding Stars
and a Constant Source of Inspiration.

Contents

Gratitude

This is an accidental book. On a long flight from Kilimanjaro back home, I had scribbled some notes about the once-in-a-lifetime experience of climbing Mount Kilimanjaro. Occasionally, I talked to my family and friends about the exhilarating adventure. Most of the discussions were in bits and pieces. After hearing new snippets each time, some family members suggested that I should write about the experience from start to finish. I didn't think I would be able to write more than ten pages.

When I started writing, one by one every day, every hour, every minute from the trip came to life. A plethora of memories came back, and the words started flowing. That is when the idea of compiling the memories in this book emerged. So first, I thank my family for encouraging me to write.

It all began with my parents. They instilled the love of nature, outdoors, and adventure in me. Both were incredibly proud when I visited them after my trip to Kilimanjaro. The love and affection in their eyes and the warm embrace were priceless to me. My Dad passed away recently, but I know he is watching - happy to see the book published and giving me another pat on the back. My brother Avinash, and sister Vijaya, have always been a rock of support throughout my life, including this adventure.

I am especially grateful to my wife Varsha, and daughters Titiksha and Tanishtha, for letting me embark on the adventure. They also had to put up with me while I spent countless hours writing and perfecting this book. They didn't have any choice in the matter but became the first readers and reviewers of the early draft! My writing - prone to mistakes - has been made better by their early and often reviews. Titiksha contributed with her writing style and language suggestions, and Tanishtha helped in creating the wonderful book cover.

Many others provided valuable suggestions for improving the book – my brother and sister, my nephews Vinay and Rushikesh, niece Radhika, friend Avinash and his wife Geetanjali, my wife's colleague Ms. Mimi, and my brother's friend Prakash. Thanks to their patience and a watchful eye, I was able to improve upon the early draft.

Words will never be enough, but finally, thanks to the real heroes of Kilimanjaro - the guides and porters who made my dream possible. As a small token of appreciation, I have decided to donate proceeds from the sale of this book to organizations in Kilimanjaro, working to improve the lives of the local porter communities.

* * *

1.   In Search of a New Goal

"When people throw stones at you, you turn them into milestones."
~ Sachin Ramesh Tendulkar ~

Life, so far, has been enriching and satisfying. In particular, the last few years were extra special. I was fortunate to be a part of some incredible events. I pursued several lofty dreams, personal as well as professional, and was able to fulfill them. On a personal level, *Matru-Pitru Sohala* (event honoring parents) during Aai-Dada's (Mom and Dad) 50th wedding anniversary in 2012, and Dada's 75th Birthday celebration in 2015 were the crowning glory of fulfilling events.

Then came November 2016 - my surprise visit to family in India and an overnight trip to Naneghat, a historic mountain fort in Maharashtra, India. Initially, the plan was to have just 7-8 immediate family members on the trek. Then a series of "what-ifs" started. What if we asked a couple of friends, or cousins, or their families and so on. My brother Avinash, nephew Rushikesh and niece Radhika went into an overdrive mode to confirm participants and coordinate logistics. The number kept swelling by the hour - 10, 15, 20. Within the next thirty-six hours, the total rose to forty-five! Especially satisfying was that Aai and Dada could accompany us on the trip. I acutely felt the absence of my wife Varsha and daughters Titiksha and Tanishtha, as they were in the United States. It was amazing that family members across six different locations chose to get up early in the morning, drive 4-6 hours and reach the starting point almost at the same time. At the trailhead, we celebrated the birthday of one of our family members, Onkar - the flamboyant traveler in our family. From there, most of us took a four-hour hiking trail that culminated on the Naneghat plateau. My parents and a few others took another three-hour scenic drive to reach the top.

The path stretched over a mountain range, through an ancient hiking trail to the Naneghat plateau. It came to prominence during the Satavahana dynasty (200 BC – 190 AD), when it was used as a toll-booth to collect toll from traders crossing the hills. During those times, it was the fastest route that linked the Indian west coast with the economic centers of the Deccan plateau. The term "*Nane*" means coin, and "*ghat*" means pass. It is also famous for an intricately carved cave with inscriptions in Brahmi script. These inscriptions are dated around 2 BC. On the fort, we explored the trading route, ancient ruins, and the famous cave. At the highest point of the pass, there was a six-foot stone-carved container by the roadside to collect tolls. It was fascinating to see these ancient artifacts, and we were left marveling about the ingenuity of the people at that time.

A sumptuous meal and some rest followed. Later, groups scattered to enjoy the scenic beauty, fresh mountain air, and a memorable sunset. After dinner, we all played games and talked about our life goals. It was an open and candid conversation amongst all. It was inspiring to hear youngsters talk about their objectives, why they chose them, and how they plan to achieve them. More activities and site-seeing followed the next day. Then reluctantly, just around noon, everyone started the return journey. A simple idea of taking a handful of family members on a hike quickly evolved into a memorable gathering of forty-five extended family members spanning three generations.

At the end of the trip, I received several heartwarming messages for bringing all the family members together. My cousin Padma wrote a beautiful letter summarizing all the sentiments. One of the messages was from my nephew, Vinay. Among other things, he suggested - "You have already fulfilled your goals mentioned during our Naneghat chat. It is time now for you to look for a new one."

This humbling experience allowed me to reflect on my life goals. At that point in life, I was genuinely feeling as complete and satisfied as a human being could be. When it came to my family, knowing the right things to do, and then being able to do them was gratifying. However, Vinay's comments triggered a background process in my head.

With family on Naneghat

I returned to the US and shared the wonderful memories with my wife and daughters. Life in the US, though, had some old and some new challenges in store. I was dealing with a few issues involving powerful but negative people at critical junctures of my life. The previous two years, in particular, were intense. I thought I was managing stress well, but it turned out to be wishful thinking. Something about the confluence of the problems quietly broke through my defenses. Unknowingly, I started bringing the frustrations home. My wife and daughters watched the struggles patiently, albeit helplessly.

Thankfully, with determination, support from family, and God's grace, I was able to overcome the adversity. The sustained fight, however, took a toll on my health. On what seemed like a regular day in October 2017, I felt increasingly uneasy and had to see my doctor. After the check-up, my doctor was concerned about my condition and sent me to the

Emergency Room. I spent a day there, going through several tests and worrying about the situation. I couldn't believe that I let my health suffer so much. Stress, as they say, is a silent assassin. It was a serious wake-up call.

After coming home, I resolved to get back to my healthy self – physically and mentally. More than anything, I wanted to set an example for my family, especially my daughters, that when life knocks you down, you must fight and get back up. What defines us is how well we rise after falling. I wanted to set a stretch goal where I would have to work hard. Even if I fell short, I wanted to taste the thrill of relentless pursuit, and in the process, build a better version of myself. In a way, I was more excited about the journey than the destination. The background process initiated after the Naneghat trip now became a dominant thought in my head. Search for such a stretch goal didn't take long.

In a seventh-grade essay about hobbies I had written - "I have three hobbies - Hiking, Hiking, and Hiking". I have developed a few other hobbies since then. However, hiking still is number one on my list! That hobby then turned into a passion and has led me to explore the world, appreciate nature and understand myself in ways I wouldn't have done otherwise. I am blessed to have been born in the state of Maharashtra in India. It is home to the great 17th-century warrior king Chhatrapati Shivaji Maharaj[1], and over three hundred of his hill forts in the Sahyadri mountains.

Sahyadri mountain range (Western Ghats) is a famous biodiversity region and home to dozens of UNESCO world heritage sites. While growing up, my favorite activity was to trek these hill forts, along with my friend Amit and cousin Nandu. Rugged mountain-forts like Rajgad, Torana, Purandhar, and Harishchadragad were our favorites. At times, other family members and friends would join us. As descendants from a line of warriors, who fought in Shivaji Maharaj's army hundreds of years ago, these treks were sacred outings connecting us with the glorious history of our land. They invoked a sense of pride and gratitude towards our warrior ancestors. That is where my love for hiking, nature and outdoors took root.

The passion flourished as I became more aware of the world beyond Maharashtra. Other places, too, started to catch my attention. As a child, stories about adventurous expeditions always fascinated me. Edmund Hillary and Tenzing Norgay's first ascent to Mount Everest, Roald Amundsen's daring voyage to the south pole, or Ernest Shackleton's heroic Trans-

---

[1] Founder of the Great Maratha empire. A great warrior, inspirational leader and skilled administrator.

Antarctic explorations – all of them transported me to a different world, a world full of triumphs, tribulations, and unknowns. I used to fancy my voyages to mountains and exotic places. To dream about these imaginary expeditions was a favorite pastime.

The favorite go-to place for a fantasy expedition? Africa, the cradle of life with an unadulterated mystical landscape! One destination there held a special place in my heart, Kilimanjaro, in Tanzania. Tanzania, the heart of East Africa, is adorned with its fertile land warmed by equatorial sun and plains that indeed are many travelers' dreams. And rising from the sunbaked savanna, just three degrees south of the equator, there is this majestic mountain, capped with snow all year round - Mount Kilimanjaro (Kili). The tallest mountain in Africa, the tallest free-standing mountain in the world, and the fourth- most topographically prominent peak on the Earth! From the plains to the icy peak, there is a path that winds its way through five different climate zones, making it a unique wonder. At the base is a warm, humid rainforest, at the top there is bone-chilling arctic tundra, and in the middle, a combination of dry moorland, heath and alpine desert climate zones. One must hike through them while adjusting to higher altitude and diminished oxygen. Body and mind get subjected to extreme conditions and many unknowns.

Kilimanjaro was just a childhood dream, a dormant distant dream. Was it time to reactivate it? Was it a worthy challenge? *"Yes!"* I thought, *"This is precisely the type of adventure I am looking for. This is my next goal!"*. It was time to turn my dream into reality. I talked to Varsha, and as 2017 came to a close, I decided to achieve the caveated goal within a year. From the Emergency Room to top of the tallest free-standing mountain in the world – in less than one year! My body, mind, and soul desperately needed an extraordinary adventure like this.

* * *

2.   Planning and Preparation

Year 2018 rolled in. First things first - at work, I switched jobs within the company, thereby removing one of the causes of undue stress. That switch was a daring adventure in itself – like jumping into a dark valley and hoping for a safety net to appear! I was relieved once everything fell into place, and I transitioned into my new role. My workplace has a well-equipped fitness center with qualified and helpful staff. The fitness center managers - Ryan and Rob - were very supportive. In early January, I met with Ryan and discussed my fitness level and the 2018 goal. He created a plan focused on regaining strength, stamina, and balance. Armed with the program, I started the work-out regimen. The first few days in the gym were very challenging, but I stayed the course. In parallel, I started focusing on diet, rest, and recovery. After a couple of weeks, I broke through the inertia and began craving for a more rigorous work-out. Endorphins were doing the trick. I could feel that my body had switched gears. Slowly but steadily, I started seeing promising results. There was a noticeable improvement in strength and endurance in just a couple of months.

In addition to training in the gym, going on training hikes is one of the best ways to prepare for Kilimanjaro. I made a list of hiking trails within two hours of driving distance and with varying degrees of difficulty. I planned training hikes on weekends. The first couple of hikes were short, four-five mile trails, with moderate elevation gain. In subsequent weeks, I chose more strenuous trails with longer distances. I hiked several challenging sections of Appalachian Trail (AT), with thick forest, rugged terrain, and beautiful scenery. One of the trails – aptly named "River of Rocks" – was an eight-mile up and down loop through uneven boulders. I hiked that trail in a heat index of over 40^0 C (105^0 F). At the highest point, there was a rewarding view of the unobstructed blue sky and a valley covered with rolling hills, green pastures, farms, and small towns. Despite the heat and exhaustion, the view was well worth the effort. I enjoyed that trail so much that I came back the next day with twice the weight in my backpack! That back-to-back hike tested my focus and endurance.

I began enjoying the process of preparing for the hike - packing my backpack the night before, waking up early, driving to the trailhead, and enjoying the sunrise on the way. On several hikes, I would be alone for hours, but I never felt lonely. Those hours gave me ample time to clear my mind and rejuvenate my soul. The feeling of being present in the moment became quite common on the hikes. It was, as if a deep dormant part of the brain would get activated, opening the pathways for a deep, meaningful monologue. Everything about the experience, the surrounding, the state of mind was serene. So many times I thought - if this is not happiness, then what is? The only missing piece was my loved ones – family and friends.

Each hike gave me valuable information about pace, nutrition, and survival techniques. I felt better and better after every outing, despite longer distance and higher elevation. Recovery was taking less time as I trained hard, ate healthy and rested well. Over the four months, I completed almost seventy miles of hikes. I experienced a variety of weather elements - heat, humidity, thunder, and rain. I came across some friendly hikers and some questionable ones. On one hike, a man was sitting in the middle of the trail, just staring at his feet and completely lost in his thoughts. Attempts to engage him in a small talk yielded no results. On another hike, a hiker was shouting incoherently at no one in particular, making strange hand gestures. It was a weird experience to meet such hikers, but it never became scary. The hills I hiked were about 2,000 ft tall, and my longest single-day hike was fifteen miles. Although the altitude was nothing compared to Kilimanjaro, it was useful for testing my strength, balance, stamina, pace, and recovery. It also gave me a good idea of hiking gear and things that I needed to be easily accessible while on the go.

Still, doing a fifteen-mile hike in a day and then resting for a few days, was way different than what I would possibly encounter on Kilimanjaro. There it was a five-day trek to go up and two days to come down. Kilimanjaro's Summit is at 19,341 ft. At higher altitudes, the air becomes thin, with only half the amount of oxygen available compared to sea level. Every step takes a lot more energy compared to lower altitude. Blood cells are starved for oxygen, and the heart works overtime to pump blood to vital organs. I knew, no matter how hard I trained in the gym or how rigorous my training hikes might be, I could not replicate the constant change in altitude and climate each day. That indeed was an uncharted territory and became part of my risk mitigation calculus. My approach centered around understanding as much as I could about high-altitude climbing, preparing well for the best possible outcome, and then planning my strategy to face the unknowns.

I educated myself on the dangers of altitude sickness. Like many situations, I put that in the "I can't control" bucket. Concentrating entirely on things I could control, I trained hard and studied Kilimanjaro as much as possible. In any situation in life, when you face challenges beyond immediate control, your mental fortitude becomes critical. Equally important are focus, clarity, and a positive attitude. You need to show courage and accept the consequences, whatever they might be. I was confident in this department. I am programmed to do my best when faced with an insurmountable challenge - or that's what I like to think!

I continued researching possible trekking routes, agencies, trekking seasons, packing suggestions, etc. After reading books, articles, and sifting through a lot of information online, I zeroed in on a reputable agency. I started corresponding with their USA program coordinator. I got all my questions answered, doubts cleared, and joined their group hike scheduled for September 26 - October 1. Which meant I would spend September 30, my birthday, at the last camp before the summit. It seemed like all the stars were aligned.

After selecting the agency and locking down the dates, I moved on to booking the flights. Most of the flights from the USA to Kilimanjaro landed in the late evening. The scheduled departure time for the Kili expedition was 7 am. While thinking about the schedule, I didn't feel comfortable starting the seven-day hike immediately after a long flight across multiple time zones. Landing at Kili airport in the night and beginning the expedition the next morning would have meant too little time for the body to adjust to different conditions. I thought spending a couple of days locally before taking off for Kili would give me enough time to adapt to the time zone, food, and weather. I decided to combine the Kili adventure with another interest of mine – wildlife, the world of African safari, where a parade of wildlife puts on an incredible nonstop show!

I did more research on the safari tour operators around Kilimanjaro. Here too, looking for a reputable tour operator with reliable experience in African safaris was key to me. After corresponding with several agencies, I selected one that seemed most reliable. Once I was satisfied with their itinerary, track record, and logistics, I signed up for a two-day safari before the Kili climb. The idea of seeing wild animals in their natural habitat, outside a zoo, sanctuary, or a TV screen, was fascinating. The Kili trip became even more exciting. Once I had the itinerary and dates confirmed, I booked my flights. My flight itinerary had two long legs – USA to Amsterdam and then Amsterdam to Kilimanjaro.

I turned my attention to packing. Theoretically, climbing Kili is something any reasonably fit person can do. Still, the exceptional altitude makes it potentially dangerous. Altitude sickness kills, and on Kili, it often does. Nearby towns like Arusha and Moshi specialize in teams offering professional support, and no one goes up the mountain without their help. The Kilimanjaro National Park Authority (KINAPA) governs all expeditions. They certify agencies, regulate climbing permits, and set guidelines for guides, porters and support staff. Anyone climbing Kili has to sign-up with one of the accredited agencies. A lot goes behind organizing a group hike, so it is best to leave the planning and logistics to the professionals. That includes rules and guidelines for packing. Each hiker is allowed two bags:

1. A daypack to pack snacks, water, jackets, and anything else required during your daily hike. Hikers have to carry their backpack every day, so the agency recommended keeping the backpack light with only essential items in it.

2. A duffel bag - All other things required for seven days on the mountain go in the duffle bag. The weight

limit is 15 kg. Fortunately for the climbers, experienced porters hired by the agency carry the duffle bag.

For a successful expedition, these constraints were essential, which meant the packing had to be very smart. You have to pack for seven days on the mountain and account for a range of weather elements and terrains. Packing itself was a challenge. How do you fit in warm weather clothes, rain gear, cold weather clothes, multiple layers, jackets, shoes, camp clothes, medicines, toiletries, snacks, camera, and so on in a 15kg duffle bag? I tried to focus on clothes and accessories that could serve multiple purposes and would be essential. Varsha and my daughters helped me a lot with their ideas and suggestions. We watched helpful YouTube videos and reviewed packing suggestions from my agency. Once I got a handle on Kili packing, packing for two-day safari was relatively easy. It was fun to involve my family in the preparation. They even joined me on a training hike to Glen Onoko Falls. The trail was rated "difficult". Going up, we had to hike by the side of a cascading waterfall. From the top, there was an incredible view of a river making a horse-shoe shaped bend around a forested hill. It was a challenging hike, but we had a lot of fun checking out the waterfalls and enjoying the beautiful scenery. As weeks turned into months, I was feeling increasingly confident about my preparation.

But there was some drama awaiting. About two weeks before the Kili departure, I started feeling pain in my left foot. My doctor said I had a grade-1 tear in one of the soft tissues near my ankle. I didn't believe him, so he slightly pressed an area near my ankle with two fingers, and excruciating pain shot up! It couldn't have happened at a worse time. I was worried about bone or structural foot issues and assumed a soft-tissue damage was relatively less harmful. But my doctor said soft tissues take a long time, even months, to heal. He suggested I avoid stretching my left foot and use orthopedic shoe inserts to support the arch of the foot. It was awkward to use the insert for just one foot, so I ordered a pair and started wearing them.

At that point, I had completed all the training hikes. I was used to the thickness of socks and the fitting of my boots. Using new inserts at that stage was going to throw the fitting off. I had no idea how that small change would affect the grueling seven-day hike - would it help or hurt? After weighing in all possibilities, I decided to use the inserts before the hike, during the two-day safari and first day on Kili. Depending on how I felt at the end of the first day, I would decide whether to continue using them.

After putting all the hard work, I was now in the final stretch before the trip to Africa. I trusted my instincts and kept my focus on the days ahead. With each passing day, there was great anticipation. I was, as Tanishtha likes to say, "Nervcited" - Nervous + Excited! All luggage checked, rechecked, and packed. Everything felt right. Finally, September 23, 2018, the day for my flight, dawned.

* * *

3.   To Africa

September 23, 2018

There was a nervous calm in the house. I got ready, did *puja* (prayer), and asked God for strength to complete the hike successfully. Varsha, Titiksha, and Tanishtha knew how important this trip was for me. They were excited but also worried about my safety. They gave me three letters and asked me to wait until my birthday to open them. Knowing I would be tempted to open the letters sooner, they made me promise not to do so! They dropped me off to the airport and wished me success. I hugged them and assured that all would be well.

Now I was in execution mode. While roaming the airport, I saw quite a few interesting art exhibits. One of them was made with pieces of glass arranged artistically displaying the words "Make Your Mark". Given the adventure I was embarking on, I thought that sign was fitting for the occasion. For the first leg of my flight, from the USA to Amsterdam, I tried to relax and not think much about Kili. On the Amsterdam-Kilimanjaro flight, most passengers were Tanzania bound tourists - some for safari, some for beaches, and some for trekking. I spent some time skimming through the Kilimanjaro book I had bought as a reference. Reading passages about Kili's history and the seven-day Machame route I was going to hike, raised the anticipation further.

About twenty-five million years ago, East Africa was a vast plain that buckled after the African and Eurasian continental plates collided. It led to the thinning crust and formation of many volcanoes. Kilimanjaro is the result of a comparatively recent volcanic activity. Around 750,000 years ago, the mountain initially consisted of three large vents, Shira, Kibo and Mawenzi, which came together as they grew in altitude. Eventually, the Shira cone collapsed and became extinct, followed by Mawenzi. The Kibo cone, however, remained active. About 360,000 years ago, long before the first homosapiens roamed the plains below, Kibo endured a massive eruption releasing a flow of black lava. The lava completely covered the old Shira caldera and created a saddle between Kibo and Mawenzi. Kibo eventually leveled out at its present altitude and became dormant. The highest point on Kibo and Mount Kilimanjaro is called Uhuru Peak (19,341 ft / 5895m). Uhuru in Swahili means Freedom.

Three peaks of Mount Kilimanjaro

7-day Machame Route with camps

The summit of Kilimanjaro was previously entirely covered by an ice cap more than 350 ft deep with glaciers covering the top half of the mountain. At present, only a small fraction of that glacial cover remains, the most visible and impressive sections being those around the northern and south-eastern ice fields.

The Machame Route is approximately 60 km (37 miles) from Machame Gate to Mweka Gate. The route, usually covered over seven days, is excellent for acclimatization, allowing hikers to "walk high and sleep low." The hike starts within Kilimanjaro's lush green lower slopes and gets gradually steeper. As the route heads toward the Shira Plateau, the trees disappear and are replaced by low brush in the heather zone. The scenery changes every day as you climb up higher. Then the route climbs high to Lava Tower before dropping and circling below the South Icefield. Here the hikers come across the Great Barranco Wall, almost 900 ft of near-vertical climb. The circular pathway from Barranco to Barafu via Kranaga is known as the Southern Circuit. From Barafu, the long, strenuous approach to the summit is made through endless switchbacks up increasingly loose gravel until it reaches a point known as Stella Point. Then the route is relatively flat for another hour to Uhuru Peak. A two-day descent follows the Mweka trail to Mweka Gate - the final destination marking the completion of the expedition.

As I was engrossed in reading, I noticed the passenger sitting next to me was getting interested in the book.

"Hi, my name is Miriam. That seems like an interesting book. Does it say anything about safaris in Tanzania?"

"Hi, I am Vikas. The book covers a lot of topics. It has basic information about safari circuits and tour operators, but the main focus is on climbing Mount Kilimanjaro. I guess you are going for the safari?"

"Yes, I am doing a two-week safari in Tanzania. The Northern Circuit as they call it. We will cover five National Parks, stay inside the Parks and experience wildlife up close. I am excited about this trip. I have been saving up all my life, and now it is going to be a dream come true! You are going on a safari too?"

"Wow, two weeks in Africa's best National Parks! That indeed is interesting. I am doing a short two-day safari. My primary goal is to climb Kilimanjaro after the safari, hence the book."

"Oh, great! Does it take the entire day to climb it? Sorry, I don't know much about climbing or this mountain."

"One day? It takes seven days - five days to climb up and two days to come down! It is the tallest free-standing mountain in the world. Because of the long trek and extreme altitude, four out of ten climbers who attempt the climb, don't make it to the top. I am part of a climbing group, and we would be camping in tents every night. I am preparing for this trek for nine months, and like the safari for you, climbing this mountain is a life-long dream for me."

"Oh, my goodness! That is an extreme adventure. I didn't know it is such an arduous trek. You make my safari sound like a walk in a park now! My best wishes for your climb."

"Both are equally exciting – just different kinds of adventures, I think. All the best for your safari as well."

We talked more about how we prepared for the trip and experiences on the way. It was good to connect with a fellow traveler. Before long, the flight attendant made announcement signaling we were close to the destination.

Around 8 pm, the flight landed at Kilimanjaro International Airport. Pretty much all the passengers were tourists, so there was excitement in the air of reaching the travel destination. Everyone seemed ready to embark on their African adventure. From the tarmac, passengers had to walk to a small terminal building. For an international airport, it was surprisingly ordinary building. All visitors had to line up for visa-on-arrival, immigration, and baggage claim. The airport staff was friendly. They even handed out water bottles to all passengers. It took about an hour to complete the formalities.

I collected my bags and exited the terminal building. My climbing agency had arranged a taxi for airport pick-up. I started looking for a person holding a sign with my climbing agencies name. For a few minutes, I didn't see anyone with the sign. It was a bit unnerving, and a thought crossed my mind – "What if there is a freak miscommunication, and no one is here to pick me up?" I shrugged off the annoying thought and kept looking. Soon, I noticed a person holding the sign. My agency had given me the driver's name in advance. After verifying his name, I walked with him to the taxi stand. With most of the passengers gone, it was dark and quiet outside. The driver was courteous and started driving to my hotel in Moshi, about an hour away.

The road was deserted, with barely any vehicles passing by. The air was crisp and refreshing. The driver knew limited English, so it was difficult to hold a conversation. Intermittently, he was talking on his phone with someone, and the tone seemed like he was arguing. At one point, he stopped the taxi by the roadside and got down. Now what - why did he stop? I asked him what the matter was, and he tried to explain in broken English. From what I could understand, he was concerned about air pressure in the tires and just checking them before driving further. While he was inspecting the tires, I scanned the surroundings for any signs of trouble. Even though it was dark, there was enough moonlight to notice a white peak in the distance. I pointed to the mountain and asked the driver whether it was Kilimanjaro. It was a funny combination of sign language and broken English, but I understood what the driver was saying. What I saw was the tip of Mount Meru, and Mount Kilimanjaro was further away. Once he was satisfied with the tires, we both got back in the taxi.

After we exited the main highway, the roads kept getting narrower. The streets weren't well-marked, so the driver was trying to guess the address. After multiple failed attempts, he called someone and asked for directions. It took a bit more time to locate it, but finally I saw the hotel sign. The street was too narrow to drive the taxi up to the hotel. The driver helped me carry my luggage to the gate and departed. Inside, I wandered for a few minutes to locate the front desk. The hotel grounds were well-maintained and inviting. I finally found the front desk and was relieved to see an attendant. Check-in formalities were smooth as the attendant was cordial and fluent in English. My room was on the ground floor, just a short walk from the front desk. It was a simple cozy room, quite suitable for the night stay.

The snack bar was still open, so I ordered a light sandwich. After a quick snack and a refreshing shower, I spent an hour setting up my phone with a local telecom carrier. After activation, I talked to my family about the flight and arrival in Kili. After a long trip, I was tired, and my eyes were getting heavy. It was around 1 am when I went to bed. I was hoping for a good night's sleep, but my mind kept wandering, thinking about the safari.

* * *

4.   Lake Manyara National Park

"Happiness is an inside job!"
~ William Arthur Ward ~

Safari Day 1 - September 24, 2018

I woke up at 5:30 am and got ready. With bags packed, I went to the breakfast area. The hotel staff was courteous and busy setting up tables. There was a lot of variety for breakfast, and the quality of the food was excellent. I overheard a staff member talking to a tourist group about a "Welcome Kili" song. I didn't understand the words, but the song was catchy. After finishing the breakfast, I approached one of the girls working there.

"Good morning. I just heard a nice song about Kilimanjaro and was curious about what it means. If it is not too much of a trouble, do you mind singing and explain what it means?"

She seemed surprised and delighted at the same time.

"Jambo! Yes, yes, sure. Let me finish setting up this table, and I will be back."

She was happy to sing the song. Taking time from her busy schedule, she began in a jovial tone,

Jambo, Jambo Bwana (Hello, hello sir)

Habari gani (How are you?)

Mzuri sana (Very well.)

Wageni Mwakaribishwa Kilimanjaro (Visitors are very welcome to Kilimanjaro)

Hakuna Matata (No worries, everything will be okay)

I recorded the song with her permission. She was quite poised and confident while singing. The innocence and happiness on her face was remarkable. For my collection, I titled the clip "Pure Happiness!" Every time I see the clip, the simplicity and pure joy on that girl's face reminds me that happiness indeed is an inside job.

I met my safari coordinator, Yosia, at 7:30 am. I had exchanged quite a few emails with him, so it was good to put a face to the name. He explained the plan for the next two days and introduced me to the driver, Amir. They put my bags in the safari jeep. To my surprise, I was the only tourist in the vehicle. Two-day safari in a private jeep all on my own! It was an excellent start to the day.

I could not see much of the town last night, but now with the daybreak, it came to life. Amir and I started talking while he navigated the jeep through crowded streets. During my preparation, I had learned common Swahili words. I got a chance to use some of them in our conversation - *Jambo* (Hello), *Habari Gani* (How are you), *Asante Sana* (Thank you), *Mzuri Sana* (Very good), *Mbaya* (Bad), *Ndiyo* (Yes), *Hapana* (No), and the most easy one made famous by Lion King - *Hakuna Matata* (No worries).

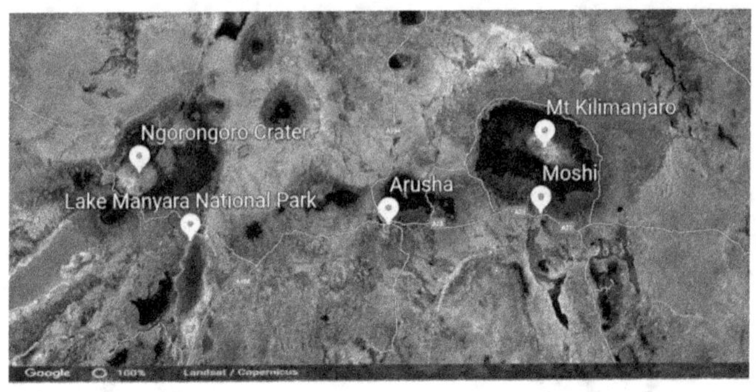

Area map with my travel destinations

Given Moshi is the gateway to Kilimanjaro National Park, most of the local economy depends on tourism. The fertile farmland surrounding the town is known for its maize, beans, banana trees, and coffee plantations. The area reminded me of my native villages back in India - Nandval and Saswad. The freshness of the air was strikingly similar. It's incredible how specific sites and senses can transport you to faraway places in a fraction of second. As we drove away from the town center, the terrain became open and flat. On our way, we passed another town, Arusha. Amir was very knowledgeable and was proud to share interesting facts about Tanzania.

"Jambo, Mr. Vikas. Welcome to Tanzania. Have you been here before?"

"Jambo Amir. No, this is the first visit to Tanzania, in fact, first visit to Africa. I am interested in learning about this place."

"No problem. As we pass places, I will talk about local culture and specialty. After the safari, are you visiting other places in Africa?"

"Oh, yes. I am climbing Kili after this. The safari was not in my plan initially, but then I decided to do it to give me enough time before the climb. Plus, it is not like I will come here often. Why not experience another African attraction while I am here?"

"Nice. Yes, many Kili climbers do that. Some do the safari before, and others do it after the climb. And then some like to go to Zanzibar for the beaches. Maybe after seeing the safari wonders for two days, you will come back for a longer safari later?"

"Who knows? Never say never! I may come back with my family in a few years."

"That's like it. Well, our destination today is Lake Manyara National Park, about 230 km from Moshi, roughly a four-hour drive. Moshi and Arusha are starting points for many popular safaris. There are sixteen national parks in Tanzania. Five of them - Serengeti, Kilimanjaro, Lake Manyara, Arusha and Ngorongoro - form the famous Northern Safari Circuit. There are over a hundred local tribes in Tanzania, each with their distinct dialect. Swahili is the national language. The Wachagga or Chagga tribe dominates large areas of Kilimanjaro and has lived here for at least four hundred years. The Maasai tribe is prominent on the western and northern slopes. They call Mt. Kilimanjaro "House of God."

A couple of hours into the drive, we took a pit-stop in a souvenir shop. The store was full of local arts, crafts, paintings, and cultural artifacts. My schedule did not have much time after the Kili hike for gift-shopping, so I had to complete it before concluding the safari. Amir said we were going to stop at a few more stores over the two days. I made a list of things to buy, purchased a few items, and made a mental note to finish shopping in other stores.

After resuming the drive, I noticed something interesting by the road-side - trees covered in blueish leaves - something I had never seen before. Amir told me that they are called *Jacaranda*. The bright-colored trees stood out against sprawling farmland in the background. Amir's pride in being Tanzanian was evident when he talked about the country's strong army, natural resources, world-renowned national parks, and mountains. Taking a diversion from the topic, he pointed at a sprawling house on a nearby hill. A Maasai village head owned the house. Rumor was that he had thirty-four wives and hundred children!

Throughout the drive, I saw several termite mounds by the roadside. Home to thousands of termites, their structure can be very complicated. Inside they have an intricate system of tunnels that serves as a ventilation system for the underground nest. The nest itself is below ground and has numerous chambers. It was the first time I saw so many termite mounds together.

It was also interesting to see the Maasai people, their characteristic huts and villages. The Maasai are famous and easily recognizable, thanks to their traditional robe, the *Shuka*. It is a bright-colored cloth, predominantly red, wrapped around their lean and slender frames. Red color symbolizes Maasai culture, and they believe it can scare off lions even from a great distance. The tribe is very traditional, and they live off the land. They rely on local herbs for medicine. They have learned to stave off dangerous wild animals just by using a stick that they carry.

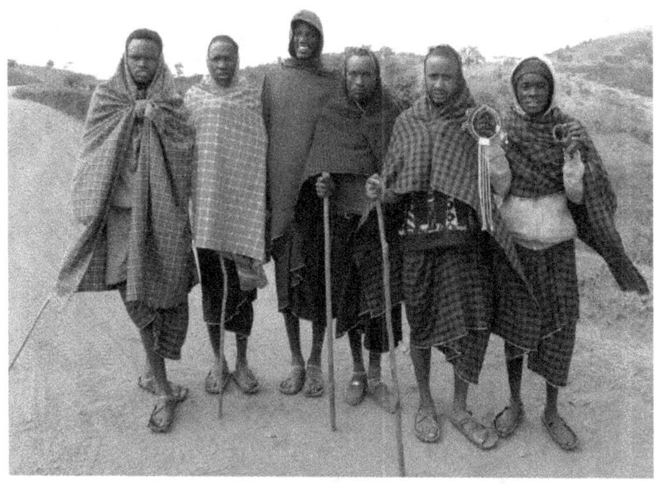

The Maasai people

Before long, we left the open fields behind and entered a small village called Mosquito River. It was named so because of the high number of mosquitos thriving in humid and damp forest nearby. Amir pointed at some unique birds and monkeys common in that region. It was a sign that we were close to the national park.

Soon we entered a large gate signaling the beginning of Lake Manyara National Park. Amir stopped at the entrance and opened the roof of the jeep. Part of the roof just slides up a couple of feet, so one can stand on the seat and peek outside. There on, it was mostly a dirt road surrounded by a variety of rainforest trees and shrubs. Immediately we came across a family of baboons. Some were big and seemed aggressive. Soon after, a couple of African elephants crossed our path. Covered in dry mud, they were busy bringing down nearby branches. It was thrilling to see such a large animal from a few feet away. The area near the park gate was full of evergreen fig and mahogany trees. Amir parked the jeep near a guard's cabin, and we had a picnic-style lunch, which he had packed in the morning. Curious baboons wandered nearby. Knowing we were in their habitat, I was careful not to attract their attention. After lunch, we set off towards Lake Manyara.

Elephant sighting from the raised roof

Lake Manyara National Park covers an area of 325 km^2 including about 230 km^2 of lake, which expands and contracts with the seasons. The shallow, alkaline lake is at 3,150 ft, and attracts hundreds of bird species. Besides the lake are extensive marshlands, saline flats, and bands of acacia woodlands. Around the lake are patches of evergreen forests sustained by year-round groundwater springs.

After navigating the rainforest, we began descending into the park. On the slope, there were native African Baobab trees. The vast grassy plains did not give any indication that thousands of wild animals roamed there freely. I stood up in the jeep with curious eyes and two cameras, ready to capture memorable images. We drove by a herd of elephants. Several giraffes peeked their heads from tall trees nearby. I saw a colony of baboons roaming the flat terrain with gazelles, bushbucks, impalas, spotted hyenas, and warthogs nearby. It was hard to comprehend the diversity of the wildlife. We stopped near a large group of grazing zebras, and I was just a couple of feet from some of them. All these animals didn't seem to be bothered by the safari vehicles.

African Baobab trees

Giraffes and Baboons

"What do think about zebras - are they black with white stripes, or white with black stripes?" Amir asked me.

"I don't know. Can't tell even after looking at them for so long."

"Many people think they are white animals with black stripes, but it is the other way around."

"Interesting! I have heard that their stripe pattern is unique to them, like fingerprints to humans."

"That's correct. Their stripes also act as a natural sunscreen and as a ploy to confuse their attackers. The predators like to attack the neck area of the prey for the decisive blow, but the stripe pattern throws them off. They can't figure out where the face or neck is."

"That's just amazing. Nature's defense in action!"

Around marshy areas near the lake, I saw many species of birds - pelicans, hornbills, crowned cranes, African fish eagle, and crested guineafowl. Amir stopped the jeep at every spot for the best vantage point and gave me plenty of time to relish the moments. At one place, several safari jeeps were parked by the roadside. All the tourists were trying to spot something. Amir asked a fellow driver and learned that a leopard was hiding somewhere in the nearby bushes. Leopards are nocturnal animals and spend most of their days resting, camouflaged in the trees, or hiding in caves. A sighting of the majestic cat during the day would be a wildlife viewing jackpot.

All eyes, cameras, and binoculars were scanning surrounding dry acacia shrubs. Amir had binoculars and started looking for any signs of the elusive animal. He kept searching for a few minutes but was unable to spot the leopard. A fellow safari driver then told him to follow a branch of a tree where he could see the spotted tail. I tried hard to look through my camera's zoom but couldn't see it. Everything in the shrubs looked the same. After half an hour of searching, I began thinking that people were just speculating about the leopard, and it was time to move on. Then suddenly, Amir found the spot and showed me where to look. It took a few more minutes and a lot more patience for me to notice the leopard's tail hanging from a tree branch. I followed it up and spotted one of the legs, then the other, and then part of his body. He was resting and lay completely still. Another branch obscured his face. At last, I was able to spot one of the most shy animals of the African wilderness. It was a different kind of hunt - and the hunt was successful!

Can you spot the leopard?

Look closely and you can see the tail!

Moving on, we reached the famous hippopotamus pool, where dozens of hippos were bathing leisurely. Beyond the pool, the Lake Manyara stretched without the other end in sight. Just nearby a few dangerous looking wild buffalos lurked almost in stealth mode. I was thrilled to see two of the African Big Five game animals - African elephants and wild buffalos. The term Big Five refers to the five most difficult animals in Africa to hunt on foot. The safari drive inside the park took six hours, and it transported me to a completely different world.

Stealth mode on!

We wrapped up the tour and headed back to the hotel. On our way, we stopped at another souvenir shop. It had some unique items, perfect for my daughters Titiksha and Tanishtha. Tonight's stay was at a hotel in Karatu, situated between Lake Manyara National Park and tomorrow's destination, the Ngorongoro Conservation area.

The hotel's location was breathtaking - on top of a hill surrounded by rolling green pastures. I didn't expect such a lovely sprawling building in the middle of the wilderness. I arrived just in time to catch the beautiful sunset. The room was clean and spacious, with spectacular views from the balcony. After taking a quick shower, I went to the dining hall for dinner. On the way, I enjoyed the magnificent sight of a near-full moon in its full glory. Far from any artificial lights, the sky was lit by nothing but the shimmering sparkle of the moon. The hotel building and the surrounding pastures were gleaming in the soft silvery glow. It was a sight to remember.

The dining hall was spacious, and the ambiance was befitting the location. There were artistic paintings on the wall depicting African culture and wildlife. Wooden tables and chairs had intricate carvings on them. Each table was separated with elegant space dividers. Soft light and soothing music made the place more inviting. The food and service were excellent, making for a fantastic dining experience. It was a perfect end to a busy day. Having had a long and hectic day, I quickly went to bed around 10 pm.

* * *

5.   Ngorongoro Crater

*"In every walk with nature, one receives far more
than he seeks."*
~ John Muir ~

Safari Day 2 - September 25, 2018

After a restful night of sleep, I woke up at 6 am, finished breakfast, and checked out of the hotel at 7:30 am. Amir was ready on time, and we left for Ngorongoro Crater. Karatu village and the surrounding area had a peculiar red dirt. It covered all the buildings, houses, and trees. Driving through that area felt like a tour of a civilization on Mars. After a short drive, we reached a large gate welcoming us to the Ngorongoro Conservation Area. The parking lot was packed with dozens of safari vans, and the area was bustling with activity. Amir had to pick up the permit from the Park office. In the parking area, I came across two safari vans with names "Mauly Tours." I am a follower of the teachings of Sant

Dnyaneshwar Maharaj[2], who lovingly is called *Mauli* (Mother). It was a reassuring coincidence, and I took it as a blessing from the Divine.

Mauly-Mauli coincidence

It was taking longer for Amir to get the permit. While I waited, a thick cloud cover began to form, followed by spotty showers. It was unclear how today's safari would turn out in such a gloomy weather. I was hoping the cloud cover would clear up soon. Next to the parking lot, there was a visitor center and a gift shop. I toured the exhibits in the visitor center and

---

[2] A 13th-century saint, poet, and philosopher from Maharashtra, India

learned interesting facts about the region's geology. The Ngorongoro Conservation Area is a world heritage site with Ngorongoro Crater as the main feature. The crater is the largest inactive volcanic caldera in the world. It formed nearly two million years ago, when a massive volcano exploded and collapsed on itself, turning it into a beautiful natural enclosure. The crater is about twelve miles (19 km) in diameter, with walls up to 1,900 ft in height. The floor is 5,900 ft above sea level, and it covers about 100 square miles. Due to its unique properties, the Ngorongoro Crater is regarded as one of the Seven Natural Wonders of Africa.

After about an hour, Amir finally collected the permit, and we headed to the crater. The road followed the crater rim for a while up to another checkpoint. We took a quick break there. Amir too was worried about the weather dampening our tour, but soon the clouds cleared up, and it turned into a bright and sunny day with excellent visibility. I was surprised to see almost twenty feet tall cactus trees lining the roadside.

Twenty-feet tall cactus tree

A nearby observation point offered panoramic views of the vast crater rim and the floor below. After the break, we continued the drive to the crater floor. Soon, we came across a herd of elephants lazily crossing the road. We had to wait until they crossed our path, but that gave me a chance to observe them up close. One of the elephants had tusks nearly six feet long. Led by this giant, the herd bulldozed small trees and bushes to make a path for themselves.

The mineral-rich floor of the crater is mostly flat and covered in nutritious grass. Large herds of zebras and wildebeests were roaming freely. Several gazelles and impalas were busy grazing. Suddenly Amir stopped the jeep near a bush and asked me,

"Do you see anything in the bush there?"

"Yes, a bush and many more bushes! It all looks the same to me. Why?"

"Look again. You will be surprised."

I looked carefully, but there was nothing but brown grass and green bushes. After a few seconds, though, I did see some movement. I watched anxiously, and soon enough, a full-grown lion came out from that bush. We were probably twenty feet from the majestic beast! The lion seemed lazy, trying to find a perfect spot for a nap. He wandered around the bush a couple of times and chose a place with most of his body covered in the shade. His face was visible but camouflaged in the brown background. The most surprising thing was there were several gazelle and baboons just a stone's throw away. They didn't care, and neither did the lion. I came to know from Amir that lions don't attack unless they are hungry or feel threatened.

Nothing but bushes here?

Look a little closer!

Further along, I encountered spotted hyenas, golden jackals, wild hogs, and vultures. At one point, I heard the sound of hooves coming from behind and becoming gradually louder. I looked back and saw several wildebeests running in unison. Amir slowed our jeep so that I could take a closer look at them. The line stretched far, and there were thousands of wildebeests following each other. As their path seemed to be cross the dirt road we were on, Amir stopped the jeep. One by one, they crossed the road in a well-orchestrated and disciplined way. Their hooves digging in the ground caused a cloud of dust in the area. It took almost thirty minutes for the entire group to cross. It was fascinating to witness that migration.

Wildebeest migration

We came across a small stream feeding its water to a nearby lake. A group of zebras was about to cross the creek when the lead zebra suddenly stopped.

"Vikas, do you see that herd hesitating to cross the stream?", Amir asked.

"Yes, I was wondering why they stopped. They were marching ahead and just seemed to notice something there."

"They are waiting for their most experienced zebra to give the go-ahead to cross the stream. The leader, based on his/her experience, gauges if there are any threats in the water. If that zebra crosses, only then, the others follow. Wildebeests also use the same strategy during migration."

I saw that behavior in action. It was an excellent example of trust and discipline in the animal world.

Approaching a small lake, I noticed a lion resting leisurely. But there was something weird about him. The lion seemed to have a mane around the face as well as his waist. Like a lion wearing a tutu! It didn't make sense, so I asked Amir what the deal was. Amir looked through binoculars and cleared the confusion. Two lions were sitting back to back, facing opposite sides. The "tutu mane" was the mane of another lion whose face was turned away from us. It is also a strategy that lions use while resting, to guard against any threat from behind. At the next watering hole, I saw another group of lionesses and their young cubs. Just a short drive from there, I saw a group of grazing hippos. Next up was an ostrich. From a distance, I just saw its neck, but as we drove closer, I got a sense of how tall and strong the bird was. It was almost nine feet tall, with legs looking like they could knock out a person with a single kick.

After a quick lunch break in the jeep, we continued towards a large but shallow lake full of thousands of flamingos. Their elegant necks and pink color against the backdrop of the wild landscape was quite a treat to watch. Nature and wildlife were at their best. These two days were a dream come true.

Lion with a tutu!

It was time to wrap-up the safari part of my adventure. Amir dropped me off at a hotel in Arusha, the base for the Kilimanjaro expedition. On our way to the hotel, I completed the final part of my souvenir shopping, except for a t-shirt and car bumper sticker with words, "I Climbed Kili". I wanted to buy that after a successful climb, not before! I arrived at the hotel by 6 pm. I thanked Amir for an unforgettable safari and gave a small gift for his family. I bid him goodbye, and he wished me luck for the climb.

My attention now turned to the central part of the adventure - Kili. I had been monitoring how my feet felt with the new inserts. They were more tight than usual, but I decided to keep the inserts as long as there was no noticeable pain. These two days gave me enough time to adjust to the time difference, about 5,000 ft altitude, local food, and weather. I was feeling good about how the plan was unfolding so far.

While checking into the hotel, I informed the front desk staff that I was part of a group starting the Kili climb the next morning. I gave them my agency's name and inquired about the local coordinator.

"Welcome, Sir. We have all your information and will let your coordinator know that you are here. They will contact you soon. Please check-in to your room."

"Thank you. I was told that there would be a pre-climb briefing in the evening with the lead guide and other hikers in the group. Do you know when and where that would be?

"Yes. Your coordinator will take care of that and let you know about the meeting."

"Okay. I had a few questions for them before finalizing the packing, so I wanted to talk to them."

"Okay, we will let them know that you have questions."

I went to my room and began organizing bags for the next day. I asked the staff again in an hour and got the same response. In the meantime, they asked me to separate luggage into two groups;

1. Kili luggage: everything needed on Kili for seven days (duffel and backpack), and

2. Non-Kili luggage - anything not required on the mountain. This luggage would be kept in the hotel cloakroom until we return.

Back in the room, I once again inspected the contents of the bags. My duffel bag was slightly below the 15 kg weight limit and had spare space in it. But I still had to pack a sleeping bag which I was renting from my agency. Generally, cold weather sleeping bags tend to be bulky and at about 2kg in weight. Without the sleeping bag in hand, I was unsure whether it would fit into the duffel. Even if weight-wise it could, what about space? It became apparent that I needed extra space in the bag to be on the safer side. After some thought, I decided not to take my bulky DSLR camera on Kili. I had one handy and powerful digital camera and phone for pictures and videos. Was that enough spare space and weight for the sleeping bag? Could I attach the sleeping bag outside the duffel? Is that acceptable? Are the weight limits strictly enforced, or is it okay if it is 1-2 kg over the limit? With no contact from the coordinator, I could only guess. It was frustrating to have such doubts the night before the hike. It was not ideal, but what else could I do?

I went to the dining room around 8 pm. The dinner menu had only one option available - a three-course dinner for a flat charge. I read the description, and it seemed like each course was a full meal. I explained to the waitress that I will pay for the entire dinner, but just need the first course. She nodded in agreement. Five minutes later, she came back with a 16-inch pizza with eight slices! The pizza was thick and loaded with cheese and vegetable toppings. I was getting full after eating only three slices and was contemplating what to do with the rest. I was shocked when the waitress brought the second course - a pasta salad, and the third course - a big carrot cake for the dessert. I was speechless! I tried many ways and finally convinced her to take the last two courses back and give it to someone in need instead of wasting it.

While I was having dinner, there was a large group sitting a couple of tables from me. They had completed the Kili climb earlier in the day and had gathered with their guides for celebration. One by one, each member stood up and spoke a few words about the experience. Without exception, everyone praised the lead guide's leadership qualities and thanked all the porters for helping them immensely, and essentially making the climb possible.

I talked to the front desk staff again after dinner. This time, they said someone would get in touch with me in the morning. I was getting agitated at the lack of communication. I asked them what to expect in the morning, what time I should get ready, whether they would weigh my bag, etc. The only response they had was to come to the lobby with all the bags at 7 am. I did not want to start the expedition on an angry note. I blocked the frustration and went to bed, trying to calm myself down.

* * *

6. The Climb Begins

"A journey of a thousand miles begins with a single step."
~ Confucius ~

Climb Day 1 - September 26, 2018

It was a nervous night of sleep. I woke up at 5 am and got ready. I took some extra time to shower, realizing that I wouldn't have the luxury of a hot shower for the next seven days. I came to the hotel lobby just before 6 am and noticed new staff at the front desk.

"Good morning. My name is Vikas, and I am supposed to leave for the Kili hike in an hour. Did the evening staff leave any message with you regarding my local coordinator? No one from the agency has contacted me yet." I asked.

"Good morning, sir. We will check into it and take care of contacting the coordinator. Till then, please have breakfast in the dining area. Don't worry."

Don't worry? I thought those words were hollow. I was supposed to leave in an hour and had no clue who I was climbing with or who the lead guide was! Every interaction in this hotel was strange. As I was having breakfast, a group of hikers assembled in the lobby with their duffel bags and backpacks. Was that my climbing group?

I quickly finished breakfast and went to the front desk. There still was no sign of my local coordinator. I was now getting upset. The staff pointed me to a room where someone from my climbing agency had just arrived. That was Joyce, one of the coordinators. Realizing that no one from the agency had contacted me, she apologized and quickly addressed my packing questions. When she gave me the sleeping bag, I realized that it was bulkier than I thought, and there was no way I could fit that into the duffel. She also informed me that I would be hiking with the group getting ready in the lobby! I rushed to my room and brought all bags out to the lobby. While checking-in the non-Kili bags with the front desk, someone asked me,

"Hello sir, is your name Vikas? Are you starting a Kili hike today?"

"Yes, I am Vikas. I just met Joyce, and she told me to get ready to leave with this group. I am still trying to figure out who the main guide in the group is."

"Oh...so you are the missing person. My name is Hermant. I am your lead guide for the climb. Sorry for this last-minute contact. Joyce told me about the miscommunication with the front desk."

"Yes, I have been trying to contact you guys since last night, and left several messages with the front desk, but didn't get any response."

"No worries, sir. I don't know what happened, but it's great that we found you just in time. Is this your duffle bag for the mountain? If you are ready, our bus is waiting outside, and we are ready to leave in a few minutes."

"Yes, this is my duffel bag. I just couldn't fit the sleeping bag inside, so it is attached outside. The bag may be a bit overweight. Is that okay, or should I transfer some items to my daypack?"

"No problem, we will take care of it. Please get on the bus once you are ready."

With a pleasant smile on his face, he took my duffel bag and asked one of the crew members to load it on the bus. I quickly completed the check-out formalities, and finally could breathe a sigh of relief! There was frantic activity in the lobby, with many people talking over each other and bags being moved around. Hermant was checking in with each hiker about their bags and directing his porters. Despite the commotion, he was very calm, helpful, and decisive.

It occurred to me that he was the same person sitting with the dinner group celebrating their Kili hike last night. When they were giving compliments and speaking highly about the lead guide, they were talking about him! I came to know later that he was in the hotel last evening, along with his assistants and hikers in my group. They had a pre-climb briefing at around 5:30 pm and went back to their rooms. I reached the hotel at 6 pm and missed the meeting by barely a few minutes. Hermant had informed the front desk that he was expecting one more hiker and asked them to call him or Joyce immediately when that person (me!) checked in. I guess the front desk staff forgot about relaying that message. They failed to make the connection when I arrived, and later, when I reminded them several times. They could have introduced me to him during last night's dinner and avoided all the anxiety and frustration I had to go through. Anyway, not the right time to think about it. One thing was clear, based on what I heard about Hermant over dinner last night, I certainly was in good hands.

There was one more bit to the hotel saga, though. As I was getting ready to board the bus, the restaurant staff came to me with the breakfast bill. I tried telling them that the fees I have paid to the agency, included the breakfast, but they didn't seem to agree. The bill was for a small amount, but the annoying part was I had packed my wallet inside the non-Kili bags, and I didn't have time to look for it. The crew was waiting for me. Joyce stepped in and asked me if I had any correspondence stating that the fees included breakfast. Frustrated, I began sifting through dozens of emails I had from my USA coordinator. Thankfully, I was able to find the correspondence to convince the restaurant staff. What a chaos! I was glad that it was over and I didn't lose my composure.

Someone called my name again. The porters were putting the last few bags on the roof, and everyone was boarding the bus. I was seeing fellow hikers and mountain crew for the first time. Not the best start to the journey, but I quickly shrugged it off and reminded myself, *"Execution mode. Eye on the prize. Don't get distracted."* I got the last remaining seat behind the driver and besides one of the porters. The bus finally left the hotel at 8 am towards Machame Gate, which was the starting point for the hike. It was about a two-hour drive from the hotel. Outside, it was a bright and sunny day with a light breeze.

After about forty-five minutes, the bus stopped at a grocery store to pick up supplies for the next few days. We all got down. I introduced myself to two hikers in the group. Both were from the USA. Dev, a pharmacist, and his friend Alberto were childhood friends and had decided to climb Kili together. I began talking to others in the group – a Canadian couple, Tim and Sasha, in their mid-thirties; Shannon from California in her fifties; Sandy from Poland in her twenties, and Owen from Ireland in his thirties. So that was the group I would be spending the next seven days with. After some small talk, Tim told me that they were looking for me last evening, and it seemed there was some confusion with the hotel staff. I told him about the comedy of errors I had to endure. It was frustrating then, but now that it was over, I could laugh about it! We chatted a bit more while the crew was shopping for supplies. As we drove towards Machame Gate, one of the porters pointed towards the peak of Kilimanjaro behind clouds. The summit was high above the clouds and looked formidable.

Reaching the top was only part of the goal. The real goal was to climb the mountain and return home safely.

We reached Machame gate just before 11 am. Nervous excitement was in the air! The trailhead was buzzing with activity. One of the guides told us that it would take some time to complete registration and permit paperwork. We had to wait for at least an hour. In nearby pavilions, several groups waited, while a signpost delivered clear warnings about the dangers of high-altitude hiking. Another sign listed name of each camp, its elevation, and cumulative distance to the Uhuru Peak. As if it was asking the climbers – "Are you sure you want to do this?!" While we sat together in one of the pavilions, I struck up a conversation with Shannon. She had recently completed her first half-marathon. Gaining confidence from that achievement, she had decided to climb Kilimanjaro.

It was taking longer to secure permits, so one of the guides told us that they would be serving lunch shortly. Having a full meal and then starting an arduous hike was a bit odd, but we had to trust our guide's judgment. The mountain crew arranged plates and served freshly prepared pasta, soup, fruits, etc. It was tempting to overeat, but we had to hike immediately after that. I ate just enough to keep me going for the day. After lunch, the guides had unique advice for us - *"Use the restrooms now. Compared to the toilets on the trail, these are luxurious!"* No one needed further persuasion to use the toilets. Hermant finished all registration formalities, came to the pavilion, and briefed us about the day.

"Welcome to the first day of the trek. I hope you had a good lunch. Today we will climb to Machame Camp, which is at about 9,500 ft. We have roughly 4,000 ft to climb over 11 km (7 miles), and it will take 5-7 hours. I will lead the group and set the pace. We have two other guides – Freddy and Goodlove. The rest of the mountain crew has already left for Machame Camp. Weather conditions change quite quickly on the mountain. We may not need a jacket during the climb, but evening and night at the camp will be cold. Usually, a couple of showers roll by in the second half of the day. The key to climbing Kili is *Pole, Pole* - Slow and Steady. Stay hydrated. This is not a race. We will take routine breaks, but if anyone wants an additional break, please let one of the guides know. We are here to help you in any way we can."

Everyone listened to the briefing intently, made the final gear check, and got ready to begin the hike. I sought blessings from Lord Ganesha, *"Ganapati Bappa Morya, Mangalmurti Morya!"*. Finally, at 1 pm, we took the first step towards conquering Kili.

Machame Gate is at about 5,500 ft elevation. For context, the highest peak in Maharashtra, India, where I grew up, is Kalasubai at 5,400 ft elevation. From the base to the top, it's about 3,500 ft climb. I had climbed Kalasubai in my twenties. Since then, I have been to many long and strenuous hikes in Maharashtra and the USA, but none higher than Kalasubai. I have traveled to higher elevations like Glacier National Park (6,000 ft), Yosemite National Park (7,200 ft), and Sonmarg in Kashmir, India (9,000 ft). The difference was I had reached those points by vehicles. So even on the first day, I was blazing a new trail in my hiking journey - starting the hike at the highest point ever.

The hike began as a leisurely walk through a winding trail up a ridge. We were surrounded by a thick canopy of trees, typical of rainforest found on the lower slopes of mountains. Due to high humidity, green moss could be seen hanging from branches. The forest was alive with sounds of birds and insects. The walk felt dramatic, like going back in time and lingering among a prehistoric landscape. The excitement and novelty of the trail were palpable. Everyone was busy looking around and taking pictures.

Rainforest

All were enjoying the steady ascent and trying to get to know each other. I learned that most of the hikers had prior experience of high-altitude treks, such as Machu-Picchu and base camp of Mount Everest. Kilimanjaro, for them, was the next step. It was interesting to hear their stories. An hour into the climb, the trail gradually became steeper, breathing became heavy, and we slowed down. We took a quick break at that point. Goodlove mentioned about a rest stop about 2 km further into the hike, where we were scheduled for a 20-minute break. After the short break, Hermant began walking by my side, and we started chatting.

"Hello Vikas, how are you doing?" Hermant asked.

"So far, so good. It was difficult not to overeat at the Machame gate. The food was too good! Does it usually take that long to do the paperwork?"

"It doesn't take that long. It just took longer than I thought to distribute the bags among the porters."

"I see. So how long have you been doing this?"

"About twenty years now. I started assisting a Kili hike coordinator while still in college. By the time I graduated, I knew I wanted to be a mountain guide. This mountain just captivated me. I joined an agency as a junior porter and then worked my way up to becoming a lead guide."

"Interesting. It sounds like you followed your passion. How many times have you climbed Kilimanjaro?"

"Too many to count! It must be over a hundred times now. It never gets old. There is something new on every climb. I get to meet new people from all over the world, and I enjoy helping them fulfill their dream of climbing Kili. It is my dream job."

"Anything that you don't enjoy in this line of work?"

"Nothing about the work itself. The only tough part is we have to be away from family for weeks or sometimes months at a time. During the busy climbing season, it just gets crazy. But that's part of the job, and I knew that before making it a career, so it's fine."

After some time, we reached the first rest stop. We were about one-third of our way to Machame Camp. Freddy showed us where the toilet was. It was a wooden structure with a door, a roof, and what could be best described as a "hole in the ground"! It was not the place to ponder about world issues while you do your business. You go in, stop breathing, do your business and come out as soon as possible!

While we rested, my heart rate settled down. It was a welcome break. After filling up on snacks and water, we marched on. As the forest began to thin out, the trail continued on a narrow spine between two shallow valleys. Now the grade got even steeper, forcing the group to slow down. Hermant assured us that we were still at pace. We might have gained about 2,000 ft by now. As we negotiated the slope and increasing altitude, most of the chatter died down. Suddenly a thick cloud cover formed, and it started to rain. Even though we were alerted at the briefing, no one was ready for the rain on the very first day.

Everyone scrambled to take their rain gear out from the backpacks. I had a poncho that covered my head, body, and three-fourth of hands and legs. Most of us got wet in the pouring rain. Lesson learned - we had to be quick in putting on the rain gear when needed. Now the trail was muddy and slippery, making every step a bit tricky. We took another break after an hour. As the rain continued, hiking boots and socks were getting wet. Even though the boots were rated water-resistant and I had sprayed water-repellent on top, they were no match for the mountain rain. It was the same situation for other hikers. Time seemed to be moving slowly. Ten minutes felt like an hour.

All along, I was trying to observe and relish the surroundings. In my mind, I was reciting Sant Tukaram Maharaj's[3] abhang[4] *"Jethe jato tethe, tu majha saangaati"*[5] and *"Vruksha valli amha soyare."*[6] Reciting these lines helped me focus on the trail and enjoy the moment. As we gained further altitude, giant heather trees, wildflowers, and shrubs began to dominate the landscape. After two more stretches of steep ascent, the tree cover began to open up. It was a tiring uphill climb. When Freddy announced that the camp was ten minutes away, we all were relieved and delighted!

---

[3] 17th-century saint, poet, and philosopher from Maharashtra, India

[4] Form of devotional poetry

[5] Wherever I go, YOU are my companion

[6] Poem expressing love for nature, plants and animals

Just before the campsite, there was a KINAPA registration hut. Per KINAPA rules, every hiker had to complete check-in formalities at campsites. It was a privilege to enter my name in the register. I decided to take a picture of each day's entry as a souvenir. Around 6 pm, we finally reached Machame campsite.

The porters had already pitched the tents. The campsite was organized in a circle, with hiker's tents lined up on one side, a dining tent in the middle. The kitchen tent, mountain crew tents, and a private toilet tent (privy) were on the other side. Our group had five hiker tents. Owen and I had opted for individual tents. Tim and Sasha were in the third tent, Dev and Alberto in the fourth, and Shannon and Sandy in the fifth. The porters had kept a sleeping pad and corresponding duffle bags in each tent. It was about to get dark, so Goodlove asked us to change into camp clothes and assemble in the dining tent in half an hour.

I had a two-person dome-shaped tent, with a small porch. The tent was about 6 ft x 4 ft x 4 ft. Although it had enough space for one person and a duffle bag, I couldn't stand inside. It had two compartments – the main area and a small porch separated by a zippered door. The porch area was good to have as I could remove the muddy boots and wet socks before getting into the main tent. Although the inside of the tent was dry, the sleeping pad was slightly damp. Since there would be no shower for seven days, I had packed body wipes. I cleaned up all sweat with them, changed clothes, and went to the dining tent. The sun was about to set, and there was a noticeable drop in the temperature.

The dining tent was big enough to accommodate the entire group, with a large table and eight chairs around it. Tim and Sasha were already there, and Freddy was talking to them about the toilet tent. It was a small tent with a chemical toilet in it. Inside, there wasn't much space to move around, so going to the bathroom was an adventure! Even though it cost our group a little extra, it was better to have the privy than using campground toilets.

Machame campsite

Our group gathered in the dining tent and began talking about the day. All felt that the first half was okay, but the second half was strenuous, made more difficult by the rain. After a few minutes, Hermant came in.

"Good evening, everyone! Congratulations on finishing the first day on time. How is everyone doing? What do you guys think about the pace?"

"I thought the pace was good, but I felt the breaks were few and long. As we get accustomed to the altitude, I would prefer shorter but more frequent breaks. In the end, the total time would be the same." I shared my opinion.

A couple of hikers in our group were good with today's break routine and preferred keeping it the same. Hermant was quick to address both inputs and talked about campsite etiquette.

"We can accommodate both styles as we have three guides, and the overall group pace would be the same. Tomorrow, we would give both styles a try. Now here is some information about the campsite. Outside the dinner tent, there are two cans of water with a tap - one with hot water to wash hands, face, etc., and another filled with drinking water. Our mountain crew boils and purifies drinking water, so you don't need to use additional purifying tablets. There is a trash bag hung outside the dining tent. No trash is to be left behind on the trail or the campsite. It gets dark quickly after sunset, so you must carry a headlamp or torch. The temperature drops quickly, so it's important to dress in layers as soon as you reach the campsite."

We had follow-up questions for Hermant. He listened intently and addressed every issue thoroughly. He seemed adept at anticipating the challenges of taking a diverse group of hikers up the mountain. While he spoke, the mountain crew brought hot water, tea, coffee, and cocoa powder along with some cookies. It was refreshing to have a hot drink after a long day. Hermant informed us that dinner would be ready shortly. After dinner, he would check oxygen saturation and pulse rate for each hiker, followed by a briefing about the next day. After the snack break, it was tempting to go back to the tent for rest before coming back out for dinner. I went to my tent, layered up, and was about to get cozy in the sleeping bag, when I heard a song playing on the radio and someone singing along with it. It piqued my curiosity. With a headlamp attached, I stepped outside.

When we started from the Machame Gate, the weather was pleasant - about 20^0C (68^0 F), light breeze, and scattered clouds - a perfect day for hiking. It was about 7 pm now, and the temperature had fallen below 10^0C (50^0 F). The rain had stopped, but it was dark and cloudy. At 9,500 ft, far from any civilization and deep into the forest, it was very peaceful. Among the passing clouds, I could see the bright moon. It was a full moon night. It would have been an impressive sight if the clouds had cleared.

The kitchen tent was busy., There were a handful of porters behind the tent, taking a cold shower from a bucket and washing their clothes. The temperature didn't seem to bother them. I navigated the campsite to reach the tent where the sound was coming from. It was Hermant's tent.

"Jambo Vikas, how are you doing? Do you need any help?"

"Jambo Hermant. I was just walking by to see who the singer in our group is! "

"Yeah, that's my hobby. I just make sure there is no one around before singing! Come on in. How are you feeling after today's hike?"

"I feel great. I think slow and steady suits my style. It's just the first day and still a long way to go."

"The first day always feels long, but it will get better. So, what made you decide to do this trek? "

"I always liked hiking and used to dream about Kili as a child. The last few years have been rough on my health, so I decided to challenge myself with this expedition. I want to regain health and show my family how to fight back. I want to set an example for them."

"That's great! I am sure your family will be proud of you. Hey, I also wanted to say sorry about the confusion in the morning at the hotel. My company is usually very good at organizing, but yesterday we had some issues with the hotel staff. I apologize. It must have been frustrating for you to not know until the last minute where your group was."

"Yeah, don't get me started on that! Did you realize, I was having dinner in the restaurant last night on the next table when you were celebrating with the previous group? We could have met there and avoided the rest of the fiasco."

"Unbelievable! Given what happened, you didn't seem upset when we met in the lobby or angry at me for not finding you earlier."

"Well, we met just in time, and you were getting the group ready. Things were heading in the right direction. There was no point in making a scene there. It didn't seem like your fault. I wanted to focus on the journey ahead, instead of thinking about what happened the night before."

"That makes sense. You have a calm head over your shoulders! I think you are going to be just fine on the mountain. We are going to have a great time."

Hermant then talked about his village and family. He also seemed to care a lot about the health and well-being of the hikers and his mountain crew. While standing there, I realized that my feet felt a little different in the camp shoes. I sat down, removed my shoes and socks, and noticed a swelling on both feet. I told Hermant about it.

"This is what I was worried about. Just a couple of weeks ago, I started using the orthopedic inserts. My physio recommended them to avoid further aggravating a soft-tissue damage I have in the left foot. All my training hikes have been without the inserts, so it's a late adjustment. I wore them during my flight and two-day safari but didn't have any issues. This is the first time I am noticing the swelling."

Having climbed the mountain so many times, he had a suggestion.

"I think on a regular walk you won't have any negative effect from these inserts. But our feet take a lot of beating on this trail. Over a long multi-day hike, feet tend to swell. You need some extra room inside the boots for feet to expand. If boots are tight from day one, your feet will hurt more with each passing day. I would suggest hiking without the inserts or tie the laces loose."

I had tried loosening the laces earlier in the day, but that didn't help. I decided to take Hermant's advice and hike without the inserts to check if that made any difference.

It was time for dinner. Everyone gathered in the dining tent. The crew served an excellent dinner - hot soup, pasta, salad, eggs, bread, jam, fruits, etc. It was amazing how they were able to prepare a wonderful meal for almost thirty-five people in such a short amount of time. It was a feast, indeed! After finishing dinner, we sat there chatting about the day.

The temperature had dropped further. As we were shivering, Hermant came in with a pulse oximeter to check heart rate and oxygen saturation. Everyone's heart rate was slightly elevated, but oxygen saturation was good. Shannon's fingers were so cold that the device did not register any reading! Anxious times, but we all passed the health-check! If these readings are outside the acceptable range, and the hiker exhibits other worrisome symptoms, the lead guide decides whether they proceed or not. The decision is made in the best interest of the hiker.

Hermant then briefed us about the next day's climb.

"Our destination tomorrow is Shira Camp. The hike will be similar to today's, but a shorter one - about 5 km (3 miles) and an altitude gain of approximately 3,000 ft. Even though tomorrow's hike is shorter, it will require more effort because of the altitude. The ascent is steeper. We will end the day on the Shira plateau at 12,500ft. Remember to go slow, stay hydrated, and don't forget to take Diamox twice a day - one after breakfast, one after dinner."

I remembered reading about Diamox and Acute Mountain Sickness (AMS) in my reference books. Altitude sickness, a mild form of AMS, typically occurs above 8,000 ft elevation. The atmospheric pressure decreases as one ascends a mountain, and the temperature drops (3-4^{0} Celsius per 1,000 ft). The body needs to deal with the reduced amount of oxygen through a process called Acclimatization. If the body does not acclimate properly, one can experience symptoms like severe headache, nausea, shortness of breath, dizziness, and muscle aches. Diamox is used to prevent and reduce these symptoms. It forces the kidneys to expel bicarbonate. As more bicarbonate is removed from urine, the blood becomes more acidic, stimulating ventilation and thereby increasing the amount of oxygen in the blood. It has been shown to decrease the detrimental effects of altitude on the body. Altitude sickness can affect anyone regardless of their fitness level. Once altitude sickness hits, the only immediate remedy is to descend to lower altitude. AMS can progress to life-threatening conditions like HAPE (High Altitude Pulmonary Edema) - fluid in the lungs, and HACE (High Altitude Cerebral Edema) - swelling of the brain.

I had put all that knowledge in the "listen to your body" and "respect nature" part of my learnings. Hermant wrapped up the briefing and told us to expect a 6 am wakeup call with hot tea or coffee in the tent.

Everyone quickly dispersed to their tents. The air was damp and cold. All the clothes I wore during the day - shirt, pants, socks, and poncho were still wet. I tried to wring out excess water and spread them on the tent floor, hoping they would dry. Even after wearing a jacket, gloves, and a winter cap over two layers, I was shivering. Getting into the sleeping bag and closing the zippers myself was hard work in itself. I think it was around 10:30 pm. After a long strenuous day, I was ready for some rest. I went to sleep almost instantly.

A couple of hours into a deep sleep, I felt that my bladder was getting full! A grave question – "To be, or not to be? Put up with the full bladder until morning, or step out of the tent in the cold night to use the toilet?" Given the effort it took to get into the sleeping bag and get warm, I decided against getting out. It meant programming the brain to ignore signals from the bladder! I must admit it was a delicate act, but the desperate need for warmth and sleep overruled the need to empty the bladder. I went back to much-needed sleep.

* * *

7.   Machame to Shira

"Going to the mountains is going home."
~ John Muir ~

Climb Day 2 - September 27, 2018

I heard someone tapping on my tent.

"Good morning. It's 6 o'clock, time to wake up."

I got up and tried opening the tent. The zipper had become hard and almost frozen overnight. After some struggle, I was able to open the tent. Cold air gushed in. Outside was Freddy, with a pleasant smile and a cup of hot water.

"Jambo, Vikas. How did you sleep? How are you feeling?"

"Hey, Freddy. I am good. How are you? It was cold, but I slept like a baby."

"Yes, it was a cold night. It will be warm soon. What would you like - tea, coffee, cocoa powder?"

"Just hot water, please. I have instant tea packets with me. Asante Sana Freddy."

"You are welcome. Come to the dining tent for breakfast at 7 am. Try to freshen up and ready by then."

"Okay. It's so nice and warm in the sleeping bag, but I will be there on time!"

Freddy moved to the next tent for his wake-up call. Reluctantly I got out of the sleeping bag and prepared my tea. The steam and aroma of the hot tea was refreshing. I could feel the warmth in my throat and stomach. After finishing the tea, I suddenly realized that I have been holding my bladder since the middle of the night. Emergency mode! I took wipes and hand sanitizer with me and got out of the tent. I was hoping no one would be in the toilet tent, and I wouldn't have to wait any longer. The infusion of a cupful of hot tea on top of my full bladder was making things desperate. It was my lucky day. Realizing the toilet tent was empty, I ran and tried to open it. Oh, the frozen zipper again! It wasn't moving at all. I kneeled and tried pulling on it, but it didn't budge. All it did was increase pressure on my bladder, the last thing I wanted. Now things were moving from desperate to disastrous! One of the porters saw my struggle, realized my situation, and quickly came to my rescue. Just a couple snaps, and he freed the zipper. I thanked him and went inside to relieve myself. I was in for a few minutes but felt like an eternity. Anyway, disaster averted. The world was a happy place again!

It was the combination of cold and wet weather, increased water intake to stay well hydrated, and the side-effect of Diamox, which makes one urinate more. Later, while talking to others, I realized everyone had their episode of the emergency. Some could wait until the morning, but others had to address it in the middle of the night. Okay, note to self - try to empty the bladder as much as possible before bed.

Simple chores like brushing teeth, rinsing the mouth, and washing face had to be done differently due to the limited supply of water. Our crew had kept a bucket of hot water for handwashing. Splashing that water on the face felt good. The sun was coming out. It was still cold, but just the sight of daybreak was making things better.

The mountain crew was busy preparing breakfast, boiling water, and getting ready for the next camp. My body was stiff, so I did some stretching and in-place jogging to loosen up. Back in the tent, I started packing my bags. Last night was a bit chaotic, trying to sort things out from both bags using one headlamp in the cramped space. I did the best I could, but things were not where they were supposed to be. Folding the sleeping bag and fitting it in its sack required a lot more energy than I thought. I changed clothes but still had few items to pack. It was almost 7 am, so I went to the dining tent for breakfast. Like last night's dinner, breakfast too was excellent - bread, eggs, omelet, cookies, hot tea, coffee, etc. Given the remote location, altitude, and the fact that everything had to be transported with the help of porters, getting to eat fresh, warm food was extraordinary.

Many of us still had some packing to do. After breakfast, there was a rush to use the toilet before the porters took the tent down. Yesterday, when Hermant had asked us to be ready by 7 am for breakfast, "ready" meant - everyone dressed for the day, bags packed, water bottles and hydration packs filled, tents vacated, and all bags outside on a tarp in the middle of the campsite! Anyway, it took us half an hour more to vacate the tents. Then we filled water bottles and hydration packs. The crew still waited patiently, and one of them asked us if we needed more drinking water before packing the kitchen tent. Filling a hydration pack with hot water required two people. The mountain crew was quick to help with that as well.

It all felt a little rushed, but it was a good lesson for us. We had to pack everything before coming out for breakfast. It was necessary for a smooth and timely operation of the daily routine. All the while, Hermant was coordinating activities, directing crew members, packing things himself, and making sure our needs were met. He was leading from the front like a seasoned General. Managing eight hikers from all over the world with diverse backgrounds, and twenty-seven mountain crew members on the expedition was no easy task. It needed strong commandeering experience and wise leadership, which he was showing in his actions.

We were asked to gather in the middle of the campsite. The entire mountain crew assembled in front of us. We went through a quick round of introductions, but these were not ordinary introductions! Each member, including the mountain crew, would come forward, announce their name and show off a quick dance move! One by one, we cheered each name and clapped to the lively introductions. It was a great icebreaker, and we got to know the names of the entire crew rather than just our guides.

Hermant again gave us a brief description of the hike and requested us to be ready each morning by the time we agreed. He then talked about a tradition where all the crew members sing and dance to traditional Kili songs before starting the day's hike. Hikers were encouraged to dance as well. What followed was a memorable Kili experience. One of the crew members, Raymond, started singing a catchy folk song with his trademark moves. The entire crew clapped in rhythm and joined him in chorus. The crew members took turns singing the next part of the song and dancing to their favorite steps! Even some of the shy ones didn't hold back. It was hard not to move to their beats. Soon everyone was dancing in synchrony. It was a great beginning to the day. The idea of such a routine was to start the day on an upbeat note before the long hike. In a miraculously short time, the porters took the tents down, organized themselves, and some already disappeared ahead, a pattern that repeated itself in the coming days. With everyone warmed up, we left Machame camp at 8:45 am.

A few minutes into the hike, we came across a Giant Groundsel tree, our first sighting on the mountain. Giant Groundsels are unique to Kili and look like a combination of burnt up cactus and pineapple. To survive in such an inhospitable environment, where temperatures often dip below freezing overnight, the plants have evolved in several ways. They store water in their stem, close the leaves when the temperature drops too far, and self-insulate through withered and dead foliage.

We climbed to the top of the forest zone and then for two hours through the moorland zone. As we gained altitude, most of the vegetation diminished in size, and the path became dotted with twisted heather bushes and Helichrysum flowers. With Hermant, Freddy, and Goodlove as our guides, we were getting lessons in Kili's wide-ranging habitat, wildlife, and peculiar plant species. Around 11 am, we took a snack break. Goodlove was carrying sandwiches prepared by our cooks in the morning. It was a nice break - sitting on rocks, admiring the views around, and enjoying a quick bite.

The trail was covered with loose rocks and dust. In a rush to start the hike, many of us forgot to wear leg gaiters in the morning. After the break, Freddy reminded us about rain gear and asked everyone to wear gaiters. As if on cue, soon after, it started to rain! We were quick to wear rain gear but lacked the tree cover that somewhat protected us yesterday. The wind also picked up. Everyone was now worried about wet clothes, socks, and shoes. We had a limited amount of clothes due to the 15 kg duffel bag limit. Cold and damp nights didn't help either. We needed to figure out how to dry clothes later in the camp.

We began talking about our past hiking and travel experiences - the good, the bad, and the ugly, making for an entertaining conversation. The hike continued on an ascending path, crossing a little valley up to a steep rocky ridge. The ridge was formed by petrified lava flow from the last eruption eons ago. By the end of the ridge, we gained another 1,000 ft. On the way, we came across incredible views of the vast valley and tip of Mount Meru rising above the clouds.

Mount Meru in the background

The rain continued. The climb became steep after the ridge making each step difficult. The trail continued north and then north-west direction, below the rim of Shira plateau. The north-west section had several rocks and boulders that we had to navigate. As a welcome distraction, there were several moorland Lobelias - elongated cabbage shaped plants that can grow up to six feet. Like Giant Groundsels, they have evolved to survive in the harsh climate. Their leaves spiral inwards, like rose petals, around the stem to insulate the water stored in them. Amazing nature at its resilient best. As if to quietly inspire all hikers how to adapt and survive on the mountain.

After another hour-long stretch, we reached Shira plateau. The temperature had dropped further. Freddy drew our attention to distinctive shiny rocks around the trail. These were Obsidian rocks, a naturally occurring volcanic glass formed when lava expelled from a volcano cools rapidly. They sure were fascinating, but the only thing we were looking forward to was the campsite. Finally, just after 2 pm we reached the Shira campsite. It was a tiring five-hour hike, but it certainly felt longer. The campground was misty, and visibility was limited. Being wet and exhausted, everyone was desperate to take shelter in tents. But no, not so fast! Hermant directed us to a registration hut to complete the check-in formalities. Reluctantly our group walked towards the Hut, which was about 100 ft from our campsite. 100 ft that no one wanted to walk!

Hikers from other groups had already queued up to sign-in their names. Some didn't have the energy to stand, so they just sat down on the wooden floor by the wall. Everyone was shivering. Water continued to drip from rain jackets, ponchos, and hats. There was another door on the side that was swinging open with blowing wind, making it even colder inside. More than a dozen people were inside, but no one had the energy to get up and close the door shut. I mustered the strength and tried closing the door, but it had swollen and could not be locked shut. I had to stand against it. The wind was gushing in through the cracks, and I was feeling the brunt of it. After a few minutes, a hiker from another group thanked me and stepped up to stand in my place. Soon everyone signed in their names and went to the campsite.

Our tents were ready with sleeping mats and duffel bags inside. Hermant, however, was not happy with something and instructed the crew to dig trenches around each tent. With a sharp rock in hand, he started digging a trench about three inches deep, circling each tent. The idea was that any flowing water would gather in the channel and flow away without getting underneath the tent. Ingenious, and something you only learn through experience! The crew had dug trenches around each tent, but not deep enough. Some of the duffle bags and sleeping mats were wet as well. It was a tough task for the porters to carry a 20 kg bag on the steep ascent in the blowing wind and non-stop rain. Despite covering the bags with a couple of tarp layers, rainwater must have found its way in.

Hermant was working along with the crew members. They quickly followed his instructions, and in a matter of minutes, all our tents had trenches dug around them. All the wet sleeping mats and duffle bags were taken to the kitchen tent to dry around the stoves. Buckets with hot cleaning and drinking water were ready. The crew members asked for our rain jackets, ponchos, hats, etc. that had gotten wet and took them to the kitchen tent for drying. Things just happened in smooth harmony. There was no finger-pointing, no shouting or yelling. The focus was on making things right as soon as possible. Pretty impressive.

One good thing about today was all the hard work for the day was over, and we had the rest of the day to relax. It was too cold to use wipes all over my body, so I had to shorten the cleansing ritual. It felt a little better after changing into fresh dry camp clothes. We gathered in the dining tent for a late lunch and hot drinks. The delicious food in such a remote location continued to amaze me. The cooks and porters deserved a lot of credit. Hermant checked up on everyone and had a quick debrief about the day so far. We had free time until 7 pm when we had to gather for dinner.

Shira campsite on an exposed plateau

The campsite was on an exposed plateau, with no trees or hills to block the blowing wind. Tonight was going to be even colder. I started thinking about how to dry the clothes. Luckily I had packed a stretch cord, which came in handy. I attached it to the inside hooks of the tent and used it to hang socks, towels, inner layers, and shirts. It was quite a sight. In the meantime, Goodlove dropped off the sleeping mat. I couldn't tell whether it was dry or not, but it certainly was warm from the kitchen heat. The rain had slowed down, but it still was misty. With the wet clothes hanging, the tent was damp. I retired to the sleeping bag for a quick nap.

I must have slept for an hour or so, but it was refreshing.

I got up and started organizing the duffle bag. I had the Kili book in the bag and spent some time revising the next few days' itinerary and what to expect on the trail. With some free time on hand, I recorded a video message for my family about the last two days' hike. The rain had stopped, and it was beginning to clear up, just in time for dinner. After dinner, Hermant came for the health check. Everyone's oxygen saturation was a little less than yesterday, and the heart rate was a bit more elevated. It was expected as we were now at 12,500 ft, and our bodies were trying to adjust to reduced oxygen. Like yesterday, some of us were shivering, and it took a couple of tries for the oximeter to register reading. The health-check confirmed that we all were healthy enough to continue.

One and a half days on the mountain seemed very long. The back to back days were tiring, but enough rest and stretching was helping with recovery. With frequent short breaks on the hike, I was able to manage my heart rate and still keep pace with the group. Over dinner, others in the group also expressed their preference for short-frequent breaks. Hermant came into the tent, asked for feedback on the day's routine, and briefed us about the next day's hike.

"Congratulations on making it to Shira camp. You all did well. So far, we have climbed in a north-west direction and gained about 7,000 ft over two days. From tomorrow until the summit night, we traverse the southern slope of Kili from west to east. Tomorrow's hike will take us to Barranco Camp via Lava Tower. We climb about 2,500 ft to Lava Tower (15,000 ft), have lunch there, and then descend to Barranco camp (13,100 ft). It's a long 10 km up and down hike and should take 6-8 hours. The net elevation gain between Shira camp and Barranco camp is just 600 ft. Still, it's an important day for acclimatization as we are going to climb high and sleep low. It will be cold, but if the sun is shining, you may not feel it while hiking. So it is best to dress in layers that you can take off and put back on as needed. You will come across incredible views throughout the day from the exposed southern slopes. Now that we are officially at very high altitude (12,000 ft - 18,000 ft), everything I said since the first briefing - *Pole, Pole,* hydration, and Diamox - is critical. Also, you have to make generous use of sunscreen and moisturizer to protect from dry air and direct sunlight. If you experience any difficulties, as always, please let one of us know. Take rest, and I will see you tomorrow morning."

It must have been close to 9 pm. I made sure to use the toilet before going to bed - bladder as empty as possible. I had one bottle filled with water in case I felt thirsty in the night. It was another cold night, with occasional wind gusting from the valley over to the campsite. With nothing but the sound of nature, the silence was soothing and meditative. Tucked in the warm sleeping bag, I reminisced about events from the last few days. It was surreal that my dream of climbing Kilimanjaro was turning into reality. Just two days into the hike, but it felt like I belonged on this incredible mountain. I thought of my family, how worried they must be now, and how proud they will be once I return. My companion for today's climb was Sant Dnyaneshwar Maharaj's abhang *"Ek Tatva Naam, Mukhi Dhari Mana, Harisi Karuna Yeil Tujhi"*. I went to sleep, reciting those words in my head.

* * *

---

[7] Conveys the importance of chanting God's name and gaining strength from it.

8.   Shira to Barranco

Climb Day 3 - September 28, 2018

It was 6 am. I heard a few taps on the tent. It was Hermant for the wake-up call. After finishing tea, I stepped out of the tent. The sun was about to rise. I couldn't notice it yesterday because of the mist and fog, but in front of me was a deep valley filled with clouds. The campsite was on the western slope of Kili. Behind the campground, I could see the tip of Kibo surrounded by its icefields. Somewhere on that peak was the highest point - Uhuru peak. The moon was still visible. The sun was rising behind Kibo, spreading its crimson glow in the sky. The cloud-filled valley now looked more like a fluffy carpet that one could walk on. It was a sight to behold.

Dawn at Shira campsite with a carpet of clouds in the background

After finishing the morning rituals, I started packing the bags, but noticed some clothes were still wet. I was running late for breakfast and didn't want to be the last one for the morning assembly. I saw Hermant walking by and called him,

"Hey, Hermant, good morning."

"Jambo Vikas. Everything okay?"

"Yes. Just have an issue with wet clothes. I am hanging them outside to dry. Might need more time to finish packing."

"Don't worry, brother. We all have the same problem. Let the clothes dry while we have breakfast. But after that, we must leave quickly. Take the jackets and other big clothes to the kitchen tent. Stove heat will help. Suggest you hang small stuff like socks, hand towels, and poncho on the back of your backpack. They will dry out in the sun while we hike. It seems like a bright and sunny day today."

That was a good suggestion. I finished breakfast and came back to the tent. It again was a struggle to pack the thick fluffy sleeping bag into a tiny sack. Freddy came to my rescue and showed me how to push the bag in the sack without rolling or folding. Indeed, experience counts! I got dressed, two layers on top and bottom, plus a down jacket, winter cap, and gloves. Sunscreen, sunglasses, bags packed, water bottles and hydration pack filled, leg gaiters on - I was ready. I looked like a warrior preparing for a battle!

After all hikers assembled, it was time for the entertaining Kili song-dance-warmup routine. It was so compelling that a hiker from another group couldn't resist the temptation to join us and started recording. We welcomed him, and instead of just being a mere spectator, asked him to be part of the action. He wasn't shy and had some entertaining dance moves himself! It was another great start to the day.

We broke the camp at 8:30 am and began the hike. The temperature was still near freezing. The day started with a steady ascent through the dry boulder-laden plateau towards the western slopes of Kibo. These boulders were lava bombs blown out of the volcano as lumps of molten rock during the last eruption of Kibo. Today's hike was different from the previous two days. There was no tree cover. We were exposed to the sun, and most of the time, we had an unobstructed view of the southern valley. For the first couple of hours, the path zigzagged, rising and falling over the slope. It started as a sunny day, but quickly changed when clouds and fog started rolling in. On and off, they stayed with us for the rest of the day. We were now on the famous Southern Circuit, which traverses the southern side of the mountain from Shira Camp on the west to Barafu Camp on the east. A couple of rocky sections were tricky to navigate as the rocks were still wet and slippery.

Boulder laden path

After gaining further altitude, we reached a spot that offered remarkable views of the Shira Plateau, our tiny campsite, and the cloud-filled valley. The view was short-lived, though, as clouds quickly blanketed the area. The hide and seek with the sun continued. After two days of mostly wet and cold weather, the warmth of the sun was welcoming. Giant Groundsels and Lobelias were constant companions now. There still was an endless barren landscape ahead waiting to be conquered, but the good news was no rain so far. With intermittent breaks, we kept taking time to enjoy the scenery. The outer layers started to come off as the body warmed up. Freddy and Goodlove were helpful and entertaining as usual. They also took on the added responsibility of being our photographers. With panoramic views and dry weather, the demand for their photography services was high. Hermant would occasionally interject and keep us on track.

Cloud filled valley

We were now going in a south-east direction towards Lava Tower. The plants that cling on here are real survivors. The soil is poor, air thin, and the temperatures extreme. The only moisture comes from mountain streams, the runoff from melting snow, and glaciers above. Among the desolate terrain, only a few everlastings and lichens managed to survive. Away from streams, the plants sustain themselves with moisture from the fog.

It was a long slog uphill through a Martian landscape. Four hours into the hike, feeling out of breath was becoming a common occurrence. We were approaching what looked like 300 ft hill. As we got closer, though, the trail dipped another 200 ft. We had to climb down and then back up over the hill! Not something anyone was expecting or looking forward to. I saw tiny dots along the path snaking up the hill. Closer observation revealed the dots to be porters and hikers from another group.

Tsunami hill

That hill just stood like a giant tsunami frozen in time! It seemed very intimidating. By the time we reached the bottom, we were dead-tired. Hermant encouraged us to go slow and steady. He showed us how to use the "rest step" method. It's especially useful for climbing at high altitude. Take five small steps, wait for a few seconds to catch a breath, repeat. I kept moving using that method. After an hour, we were finally on top of the hill. It certainly felt longer than that. As we approached Lava Tower, the fog became thick. It looked like the dry spell we had experienced since morning was about to end.

Lava Tower, also known as Shark's Tooth, is a large 300 ft tall rock formation formed when

Kilimanjaro was still an active volcano. In geological terms, it is a volcanic plug. During the last eruption, lava shot out of a vent at the base of where Lava Tower now stands. In time it cooled and hardened, thus "plugging" up the vent beneath.

At a little over 15,000 ft, this was our lunch stop today. We all needed a break after the exhausting hike. Porters quickly set up the dining tent while we completed check-in formalities at **KINAPA** registration hut. While in line, I met a hiker who was doing the climb for the third time. He was so intrigued by Kili that scaling it once wasn't enough. I tipped my hat to his enthusiasm.

Lava Tower camp

We finished lunch in an hour. I noticed that none of us could eat much. I couldn't figure out whether it was because of the tiring hike, cumulative exhaustion, food, damp surroundings, or the altitude. It was the highest elevation for the day, and now we had to descend into Barranco Valley. After climbing up so much, any hike that was "not uphill" was cheered upon. But Hermant asked us to be careful, as going downhill puts extra stress on knees and legs, which were already fatigued.

Just in time for the next stretch, it started raining. It made the rocky trail slippery and precarious. I soon realized it was challenging to descend while wearing a poncho. The loose portion of the poncho kept blocking the view directly below my feet. At many places, I had to use both hands and feet to step from one rock onto the next. That 300-400 ft rocky section certainly warranted extra caution. After that, it was a relatively gentle downhill path towards Barranco Valley. The valley is a large groove in the southern face of Kibo. It was formed by a massive landslide that swept down from the top thousands of years ago. It is also called the "Garden of the Senecios" due to the abundance of Senecio (Kilimanjari) plants. The plant forks as it grows. Each branch grows for twenty-five years, flowers and forks again. It's another twenty-five years until the next flower. The dead leaves serve to protect and insulate the trunk.

By the time we reached the camp, we had climbed up roughly 2,500 ft and descended about 2,000 ft. Numbers alone didn't tell the entire story. It required a lot more effort than what the numbers suggested. The altitude certainly had something to do with it! It was around 5 pm, and the drizzle had stopped. I noticed some new crew members in the camp. Wondering who they were, I asked Raymond.

"Are the new people from another climbing group?"

"Oh, they are from our group. They just climbed up to drop off a fresh supply of groceries, fruits, and other camp material for the rest of the expedition. They will spend the night with us and go down tomorrow. When we started, we pack supplies that last for three days or so. Fruits, vegetables, poultry don't stay fresh longer, and we also have the 20 kg per porter limit, so we can't carry more supplies from the beginning."

"Wow! Did they come all the way from Machame?"

"No, that's a long route. They came up by the Umbwe route, which is a shorter route but has steep ascent. It climbs roughly 8,000 ft over eleven miles. Since the route climbs so quickly, only experienced climbers use it. We don't allow some of our new porters to come through that route."

"That's incredible. Such a steep climb in a day with heavy bags with them! They must be extremely fit for this altitude."

"Yes, some of the fittest porters indeed."

Since the first day, I saw how hard the mountain crew - porters, cooks, and guides - were working. The porters hiked twice as fast, with each one carrying a 20 kg bag. Food, water tents, medical supplies, and clothing for five climate zones had to be carried up, and every scrap of waste had to be carried down. Their typical day was hectic and demanding. Get up early by 5 am, fetch water from nearby streams, boil and purify it for everyone, fill buckets with hot water for hikers, prepare breakfast, lunch, dinner for thirty-plus people, pack-unpack-setup all tents, clean dishes, carry all campsite material, food supplies, toilet tent, emergency equipment and more on their backs, help out hikers with any issues, and so on. All of it, without complaining and with reliance on each other for teamwork, camaraderie, and flawless execution. Language barrier or not, they were always willing to help us with a smile. It was a great testament to their professionalism, character, endurance, and superhuman strength. Most of them were young men in their twenties with a lean but fit physique. The guiding force behind the unit was Hermant, an inspirational leader. It was great to see such a cohesive unit and Hermant's efforts to treat them as equals. He kept the young bunch intact, marching towards the same goal. There are very few instances in life when one gets to witness simplicity and greatness blended like this.

Tents were pitched, and the sun was about to set. We sat in the dining tent for hot drinks and snacks. The conversation among the group was not as cheerful as it was in the last two days. Maybe it was the fatigue setting in after three days on the mountain. Exertion, sanitation, harsh weather, and altitude may have been the compounding factors. In my mind, it all was part and parcel of the expedition, and there was no point in complaining.

After snacks, I stepped outside the tent to catch up with the mountain crew. While talking to them, a jagged rocky wall behind our campsite caught my eye. It was covered in the orange glow of the setting sun. I learned from a nearby porter that it was the famous Barranco Wall, also called the Breakfast Wall. It would be the first thing hikers tackle the next morning on the way to Karanga Camp. The wall showed geological scars from the massive landslide, which resulted in the formation of Barranco Valley. It is about 900 ft of near-vertical scramble, which stands in the way to the peak. As if to test the hikers' mettle and grit before allowing them passage to even tougher challenges ahead.

Three long days in, four more to go. I was doing fine physically. My body was sore, but nothing to be concerned about. Removing the inserts from the boots seemed to be the right decision. Swelling in feet had subsided, and the troublesome left foot was not bothering me anymore. I had stopped stretching that ankle to prevent aggravating the soft-tissue injury. All the hard work I had put in over the last several months was paying off. Every day I did stretching in the morning and evening, which helped in reducing the soreness. Above all, my mind was fresh, focused on enjoying the journey, and keeping an eye on the ultimate goal.

After dinner, day's recap, and a health-check, Hermant talked about the importance of having enough calories as the physical demands increased by the day. He briefed us about tomorrow's hike to Karanga Valley Camp. It would be a comparatively shorter distance, about 3.5 km, but expected to take four to five hours. By now, I knew not to be fooled by "shorter" distance! The higher you climb, every step becomes more strenuous. It would be about 1,500 ft up and down hike with no net elevation gain. The highlight for the next day, of course, was scaling the Great Barranco Wall. The weather was expected to be the same as today.

It was dark by the time we came out of the dining tent. As I was walking towards my tent, I happened to look up. It was a completely different world, filled with countless stars in the sky, like I had never seen before. And a big bright moon illuminating everything around it. I turned my headlamp off. The full moon was two nights ago, so the splendor of its glow was still near its peak. The Barranco wall stood silhouetted against the deep velvety sky. Millions of stars twinkled against the backdrop. The moonlit sky seemed like an ocean of glittering stars. I felt so insignificant and far from the massive expanse above. But at the same time, it felt like I could touch the stars and be part of the expanse. It was a memorable and awe-inspiring sight. A surreal experience indeed!

It was difficult to take my eyes off the sky, but the falling temperature forced me to take shelter inside the tent. The soft shimmering glow of the moon gave me a sense of direction in what would otherwise have been a maze of impenetrable blackness. With day three under the belt, I was excited about being closer to the goal. I quickly went to sleep dreaming about the night sky and millions of stars above.

* * *

9.   Barranco to Karanga

Climb Day 4 - September 29, 2018

I got up before the 6 am wake up call. The ground outside the tent, the tent lines, and zipper were covered in icicles. My body was stiff due to curling into the sleeping bag all night long and trying to stay warm. Coming out of the tent in the bitter cold was a shock to the senses. I did some stretching to warm-up and got the blood flowing. The sun was about to rise as I could see the horizon beginning to light up. Brushing teeth and washing face had a different feel today. As usual, the crew kept a bucket of hot water available, but as soon as I splashed the water on my face, it turned cold in an instant. My hands and face felt frozen in seconds. It was day four without a shower. This is when you realize how luxurious it is to have running hot water for daily chores! Three more days of this, I told myself, and carried on with the routine.

Talking to Freddy, I learned that Owen couldn't sleep most of the night because of a severe headache. It was the first sign of AMS in our group. Lack of sleep and headache at this altitude was concerning. Hermant checked upon him and gave him medicine. Owen seemed to feel better in the morning, and after consultation with Hermant, decided to continue. After the song-dance-warm up routine, we began to march towards the Barranco Wall at 7:30 am.

The idea of climbing the wall first thing in the morning was daunting. It was a 15-minute walk through the valley to reach the base of the wall. The beginning was deceptively gentle. I could see a line of porters dotting various sections of the wall. It is the toughest part for the porters to climb with heavy sacks on their heads. The tiny dots ascending the wall gave a sense of its sheer size. It looked like a guardian fortress blocking our path to the coveted goal. Hermant asked us to watch out for black ice on the rocks and make sure we use both hands and feet throughout, to scramble up the wall. The trick was to climb slowly, making sure of each foothold and handgrip.

The Barranco Wall

I took my time to navigate the first few minutes of the scramble to get a sense of how slippery the rocks were. The sun was coming out, and although it was still around freezing, the warmth was enough to melt the ice that had formed overnight on the rock face. It was difficult at first, but once I got the hang of how to avoid the slick spots, it became easier. I would almost prefer this type of scramble than a relentless uphill climb. Not everyone in the group was comfortable on the wall, though. There was always the danger of loose rocks being accidentally rolled down by climbers ahead of you. A couple of group members slipped on the rocks, but luckily there were no injuries. Freddy and Goodlove took backpacks from struggling members so that they could climb without any weight. Hermant, as usual, had a watchful eye on everyone's movement. He showed me the right places for foothold and handhold. He would warn me about icy patches, and I would then relay the warning to the person behind me and so on.

The wall was the only place on Kili so far that had a significant exposure. It wasn't a place to miss your footing. A small mistake could result in a severe injury or even death. Steep, narrow paths cut back and forth along the rock face, making it a challenging section of the mountain. Although difficult, it does not require any technical climbing skills or equipment. Taking your time and being mindful of where you place your hands and feet is essential. We kept taking short breaks for everyone in the group to catch up. The views of the valley kept getting better and better as we gained altitude. I was enjoying the climb as it wasn't taxing my heart rate as much.

At one point, we came across a famous spot on the wall called the "Kissing Rock." It's a narrow section with a bulge in the rock. You must pass it by clinging to it with both hands, with your back to the valley. Because of the tight space, you almost hug the rock, creating an intimate experience. To make it more memorable, many climbers opt to kiss the wall and add a little spice to the adventure. A couple of challenging sections followed the Kissing Rock. The guides had to carefully pull each of us up due to loose gravel and lack of any footholds. Finally, in one and a half hours, we conquered the wall. A significant challenge overcome, and as a result, we were rewarded with incredible views. Clear blue sky, bright sunshine, Kibo's icefields over the shoulder, a cloud-covered valley in front, and the tip of Mount Meru peeking above the clouds on the right - it was by far the most scenic spot on Kili yet.

View from the top of the Barranco Wall

We celebrated the accomplishment and took our time to take in the magnificent panorama around us. After the break, the trail continued on a descending path covered in loose gravel, typical of the alpine desert zone. From the bottom of the gully, I could see a long desolate path snaking up and down through the hills. Fern, heather, and other bushes reappeared as we descended into the valley. From there, it was about an hour's steep ascent to the Karanga campsite. The last uphill climb caught all of us off-guard. We were not supposed to gain any net altitude today, so after climbing a 900 ft wall first thing in the morning, the assumption was it was all downhill to the camp. But, on the way, we passed through a few more hills and valleys with a net drop in altitude. After the physically draining climb, we were at 13,100 ft - almost the same elevation as the last camp!

We reached the campsite at about 1 pm. We didn't have rain throughout the day, and most of the wet clothes had dried during the hike. The best part was we had the remainder of the day to rest and acclimatize. Just when we were rejoicing at the prospect of doing nothing, Hermant burst our bubble.

"Team, you did good today. We have the rest of the day at our disposal. We will have lunch and some rest. After that, if the weather cooperates, I suggest we go on an acclimatization hike up the ridge behind the camp. It will be a short, one-two hour hike."

"Is it absolutely required? It's been a long day already. Can't, we take rest and maybe do some warm-up activities at the camp later? It's going to be tiring to put on the hiking gear again just for a couple of hours." One of us expressed the group's sentiment.

"It will help you to be as ready as possible for the summit. You don't need the full hiking gear, just a bottle of water, a couple of warm layers, and a headlamp just in case it gets cloudy before the sunset. It's up to you if you want to carry a backpack. The main goal of the hike is to gain 200-300 ft elevation, come back and let your body continue to acclimatize."

We exchanged glances, and it was clear that no one was in the mood for another hike. We pinned our hopes on "if the weather cooperates" part. For the first time on the mountain, I was secretly praying for rain! On a practical level, the hike made sense as it gave us the best chance of success for the final push.

The mood during lunch was similar to yesterday. The group was getting edgy. Most of us had lost appetite. It seemed like every day we were eating the same food. Whenever I could, I tried to lighten the mood and change the subject to focus on the positives.

After lunch, I went back to the tent, wrote a few notes in my diary, recorded a message for my family, and surrendered to the sleeping bag for a post-lunch siesta.

Freddy came calling around 4 pm and told us to get ready for hot drinks followed by the hike. I looked outside, hoping for clouds and rain, but my wish remained unfulfilled. After some snacks and tea, we started the acclimatization hike. It was a moderate ascent on a hill behind the camp. Hermant led us on the hike at a comfortable pace and kept us busy in wide-ranging conversations. His affection and reverence towards Kilimanjaro was a recurring theme. Other topics included Tanzania history, world events, international politics, customs, and cultures. It was impressive to see his breadth of knowledge and willingness to learn about different cultures.

"Vikas, I have heard you say something at the beginning of every day. Some sort of a chant. Why do you say that?" Hermant asked me.

"You mean, *Ganapati Bappa Morya, Mangalmurti Morya?*"

"Yes, yes. What does it mean?"

"In Hinduism, we revere Lord Ganesha as the God of intellect, wisdom, and good luck, as well as the remover of obstacles. It is common practice to seek His blessings before starting the day or any important activity. That's what you heard me saying frequently."

He intently listened to me and practiced saying *"Ganapati Bappa Morya"* along with me. The rest of the group joined in the chorus as well. It was a special feeling to hear the sound reverberating on the hill. We talked about family and various customs about respecting nature. Hermant then spoke about a tradition the Chagga tribe has been following for thousands of years.

"The Chagga families have a strong communal bond. We not only care for the immediate family, but also contribute to the well-being of the village. There is a great deal of focus on maintaining peace and harmony among each other and with nature. If there are any disputes within the community, we have a custom of offering a Yucca plant."

"What is the Yucca plant? The custom sounds like offering an olive branch." I asked.

"Yes, similar. We use the leaves for weaving, healing, and as a symbolic means of settling disputes, much like the offering of an olive branch. The recipient cannot decline the offering as it has spiritual significance, making the offering a very effective means for mending fences. You will see Yucca plants outside almost every house."

"That's quite interesting. Your forefathers indeed were wise and knew how to maintain peace."

He also talked about an incident on Mt. Kinabalu in Malaysia. There was an earthquake near the mountain, which killed sixteen hikers in the summer of 2015. Locals believe Mount Kinabalu is the final resting place for their ancestors and is a sacred mountain. A few days before the earthquake, a group of western hikers had stripped and posed naked on the mountain. Their local guide tried to stop them from doing so, but they hurled abuse at him. Locals were enraged at the disrespectful behavior. The day before the quake struck, some locals saw a flock of birds unusually circling the area and took it as a bad sign. Some believed the earthquake was a result of the disrespectful behavior of the tourists. Others completely dismissed any connection. Most people, though, agreed that local beliefs and customs should be respected.

The acclimatization hike took less than two hours but was filled with meaningful conversations. It struck me how fundamental human values - selflessness, taking care of family, taking care of each other, respecting elders, and cultivating nature - transcend time and boundaries. As long as humans remember and act like one species, these core values would stay alive.

Our return to camp couldn't have been timed any better. The sun was setting on the horizon. With no obstructions and endless visibility, the sky and earth seemed to have merged, creating an infinite expanse. The sun was unleashing its magic by spreading vibrant hues of gold blended with orange and crimson. On the right, there was a small rocky outcrop silhouetted against the backdrop. Way in the distance, the tip of Mount Meru stood above a layer of clouds. Behind me was the southern face of Kibo with its icefields basking in the orange glow of the sunset. The shades in the sky changed every second like a master painter skillfully mixing colors from his palette. It was a mesmerizing sight to witness, a sight capable of enriching the soul and transporting me into timeless existence. Time stood still, and I felt a sense of being one with nature. The mystical location, unforgettable scenery, and the enchanting sunset made Karanga my most favorite camp on Kili.

Kibo peak

Breathtaking sunset

A quick dinner, health-check, and briefing followed. Everyone dispersed to their tents. The next morning, we would be climbing to Kosovo camp via Barafu. At 15,500 ft, Kosovo would be our highest and final camp. We had about 2,400 ft elevation gain over 3.5 km, and it was estimated to take four-five hours to hike. As darkness quickly blanketed the sky, the temperature dropped significantly. I wrapped up one of the most eventful days on Kili and surrendered to the comfort of the sleeping bag.

* * *

10. Karanga to Kosova

Climb Day 5 - September 30, 2018

Surprise, surprise...it's my Birthday! No one knew about it yet. With images from last evening's sunset still fresh in my mind, I got up at 6 am, and finished the morning chores. We had planned to start today's hike by 7:30 am, to give enough time for rest before the summit bid later in the night. I had packed a bag full of treats and chocolates for the entire group as a birthday surprise. Just before vacating the tent, I took the bag out from the duffle and went to Hermant.

"Hermant, before we leave, I have a request for you. I have a bagful of chocolates and would like to distribute to the entire crew."

"Chocolates, great! Good for energy. But why now, is there anything special?"

"Yes, it's my birthday today."

"What? And you are telling me now? Come on! You should have told me earlier. We could have planned a nice celebration today."

"Well, last night, everyone was so tired, and I really wanted to give a surprise."

"Okay, no problem. We will make NOW a perfect time."

He gathered everyone in a circle and announced that it was my birthday. Everyone was surprised and gave me a hard time for not telling them earlier. While I was handing the treats to each crew member, Hermant and Freddy quietly sneaked to the kitchen tent and came out with a lighted candle on a plate. I was at the center of the celebration now. I blew out the candle, and everyone sang *Happy Birthday*. Their wishes echoed back from the mountain face and seemed to evaporate in the valley. It was as if Mother Nature had joined the chorus in wishing me. Special, truly special!

We continued the celebration for a few more minutes. I preferred a quiet, low-key birthday celebration, but was touched by Hermant's kind gesture and everyone's wishes. I realized that it brought a smile on everyone's face and was a good distraction from the daily grind. Getting to celebrate my birthday during a once-in-a-lifetime adventure was exceptional. It was, and still is, one of my most memorable birthdays ever!

We began the hike at 7:30 am. It was the same steady uphill trail that we walked last evening for the acclimatization hike. We were at the tail-end of the southern circuit. We started walking in the north-east direction just below Kersten and Decken glaciers. The landscape was as desolate as yesterday - loose rocks, boulders, and gravel were scattered everywhere. As we steadily gained altitude, every step became increasingly difficult. Our pace slowed down, and the frequency of breaks increased. After a couple of hours into the hike, the southern icefields on Kibo became more evident. We now had the first glimpse of Rebmann glacier, a glacier we would be walking by tomorrow on the way to the Uhuru peak.

Alpine desert

Fatigue, altitude, and the steep ascent made the 3.5 km hike feel more like a 35 km grind. We crawled to Barafu camp just before noon. Barafu is referred to as "High Camp," and most groups make it the last camp before the summit. We were fortunate that Hermant had secured a permit for Kosovo camp, about 400 ft higher than Barafu. It took us one more hour to reach Kosovo camp. On the way, we had to scramble up a couple of steep rocky sections. The final stretch was torturous, but there was an upside to setting camp at Kosovo. For the final push, we would not have to climb the rigorous one-hour stretch in the night using headlamps.

Desolate path

Lunch was quickly set up in the dining tent. Hermant reiterated the importance of consuming enough calories, as there would be significant demand for energy during the grueling ascent. Reluctantly, we tried to eat as much as possible, but it was clear from the leftovers that we didn't eat enough. Sentiment among the group was more of exhaustion than excitement about the summit ascent. Most of the discussion centered around the desire to get off the mountain as soon as possible. I was equally tired but tried to change the vibe.

"We all are tired, but now is the time to reset our mind back to the first day. We climbed 4,000 ft that day. Our final ascent is roughly the same. We must hit the reset button, try to forget everything that happened over the last five days, and think that tomorrow is our first day. We have come all the way here, and our bodies have been resilient. It's just our minds that we need to put back in control. Another way to think about it is, after the final eight-ten hour climb, we will be on Uhuru peak, and there will be no more climbing left."

I don't know how much it helped them, but I certainly hit the reset button and was looking forward to the summit bid. We finished lunch on that upbeat note. Hermant then briefed us about the plan for the rest of the day. It was the "go-time" briefing...

"Congratulations, everyone. Over the last five days, you have hiked almost 25 km, and we are now at 15,500 ft, just 3,850 ft from the peak. You have done very well to reach this point. Most people in the world will not get an opportunity to be at this altitude in their lifetime. This is our last camp before the summit. In about twelve hours, just around midnight, we will start our ascent. Until then, there are some essential things you must focus on - eating well, staying hydrated, resting, and preparing for the final ascent.

After lunch, organize all your warm clothing and keep it accessible for the night. It's better to do that when we still have daylight left. You will need four layers on top and four layers on the bottom. As you climb, the body will warm up, and you may not need all layers. They should be easily removable. Wear two layers of socks, two layers of gloves, a warm winter cap, bandana, or balaclava. Feel free to use chemical warmers if you have them. It is crucial to protect fingers, toes, and face from the risk of frostbite.

You will only carry your backpack to the summit. Keep it as light as possible. Check your headlamps and have a few extra batteries or a spare headlamp. Carry at least three water bottles. Porters will fill them with boiled, purified water just before our departure. Keep the filled water bottles upside down in your backpack, as water freezes from top to bottom. If you have a hydration pack, plan on drinking that water before using the water bottles. Hydration pack tubes may freeze, and you may not be able to drink from them. The temperature will be below freezing, at least until sunrise. Keep any cameras or phones inside your jackets as close to the body as possible, so they stay warm. Use a generous amount of moisturizer on your face. If you need anything, please ask me, Freddy or Goodlove.

We will have an early dinner at 6 pm. After dinner, we will do a gear check. Then you rest for a few hours. Even though it may be difficult, I suggest getting some sleep. Porters will stay at this camp with your duffel bag and other belongings. There will be a wake-up call at 10 pm. After light snacks, we will have a final check and warm-up. The plan is to start the ascent just after midnight, reach Stella Point (18,830 ft) by sunrise, Uhuru Peak (19,341 ft) by 8 am, and back to Kosovo camp (15,500 ft) by noon. It's going to be at least a twelve-hour slog - approximately 4.5 km and 3,850 ft of ascent, and same on the way down. Upon our return from the summit, we will have lunch break here, and immediately continue descending for another 7 km to Mweka Camp at 10,200 ft. It is by far the longest stretch of the Kili expedition, with a total of 3,850 ft of ascent and 9,000 ft descent totaling 16 km. Total hiking time will be anywhere from 14 to 18 hours. Lunch break at Kosovo camp will be a couple of hours. This will be the most physically and mentally challenging day of the hike. Depending on our group's pace, we should be at Mweka Camp in the evening for a celebratory dinner. Do not hesitate to ask for help or ask any of the guides to carry your backpacks. We are here to help and support you."

There was a nervous calm in the tent. Hermant addressed all the questions from the group. The realization that we are in the final stretch was hitting us now. Our daily routine, which we were used to for the last five days, was going to be completely disrupted. I finished lunch and went back to the tent. On the way, we saw a helicopter making rounds. Goodlove asked around and told us that a female climber needed an emergency evacuation. She was a seasoned climber and had attempted the summit last night. Unfortunately, she was forced to return from Stella Point due to altitude sickness. She seemed disoriented and had to be carried down to Kosovo Camp, to aid relief from AMS symptoms. Her condition did not improve, so an emergency air-rescue was underway. We felt terrible for her. It was a stark reminder of what altitude sickness can do. It also served as a warning sign that one needs to listen to their body and learn when to stop.

Giant Kibo was towering above us. The mystical cap of ice that rose so magically from the plains was now within reach. There was a potent mix of emotions - excitement, nervous anticipation, and a profound sense of awe. Back in the tent, I organized clothes as per the instructions, and slipped into the sleeping bag for a quick shut-eye. The countdown had begun.

I woke up at 6 pm. It was about to get dark, so I packed my bags, wore three layers, and went to the dining tent. None of us could eat much, since we just had lunch a few hours ago. We tried our best and finished dinner quickly. Health-check revealed lower oxygen saturation and a higher heart rate for everyone. Still, we all were within the acceptable range. Owen did not exhibit any AMS symptoms that bothered him earlier. Hermant checked with us to confirm proper clothing and gear. Most climbers had everything in order. A couple of headlamps were not working, so he provided replacements. I went back to the tent, waiting for the 10 pm call.

It was the calm before the storm. The anxiety was palpable. I wore two layers of woolen socks and adjusted the fitting of my boots. Next up was my outermost layer, the down jacket. I tucked my digital camera and phone in the inner pockets. Placed neatly folded Indian national flag, and Chhatrapati Shivaji Maharaj's *Bhagava* flag, inside another pocket. Outer pockets contained pictures of my deities and family. Now there was just one more important thing remaining – reading the letters that Varsha, Titiksha, and Tanishtha gave me for my birthday.

Birthday letters!

I opened the envelope and started reading the letters. The birthday wishes and heartfelt messages put a smile on my face. As I kept reading, my heart filled with emotions and eyes teared up. Here are some of the words from the letters:

"I am so proud of you for doing this! You have and will always inspire us. We all know you are going to make us proud" - Tanishtha

"Bro, I am so excited for you! Have a dope time and learn a lot of Swahillian so that I can add it to my Gangsta vocab. Love Ya!" – Titiksha. (You guessed it right. She is my teenage daughter!)

Both wanted me to try local food and bring some favorite dishes back home!

"May God grant you the strength to achieve and fulfill your dreams! The best view comes from the hardest climb." - Varsha

She also had two quotes from my mountaineering heroes:

"It is not the mountain we conquer but ourselves." - Edmund Hillary

"The mountains are calling, and I must go." - John Muir

The letters meant a lot to me. I realized that they must be missing me and anxiously waiting to hear the updates. Their love and words of encouragement strengthened my resolve to conquer the Uhuru peak, and return home safely. I tucked the letters back in the envelope and went to sleep.

It was 10 pm. Even with multiple layers, I was shivering inside the tent. I applied moisturizer on my face, ears, and neck. Wore thick winter pants over the two bottom layers, put on the down-jacket, covered my face with a balaclava and a warm winter cap, covered my hands with liner gloves and thermal winter gloves. I kept chemical warmer packets inside gloves and socks. With hiking poles attached to the backpack, headlamp on, and gaiters fixed, I was ready. Everyone gathered inside the dining tent.

Hermant again went through the step by step instructions. We had light snacks and hot chocolate before stepping outside. It was dark, cold, and dead silent. Nothing was visible beyond the headlamp beam. Not many in our group had hiked through a night. It was going to be an adventure in itself. Porters brought hot water and helped us fill water bottles and hydration packs. We did warm-up drills. Hermant,

Freddy, and Goodlove were ready as well. We waited
for the signal to start the climb.

* * *

11. Kosovo to the Summit, and Back to Mweka Camp

Climb Day 6 - October 1, 2018

It was just after midnight. *"Ganapati Bappa Morya, Mangalmurti Morya!".* The chants marked the beginning of the summit ascent. We wished each other luck and began the quest to conquer the highest freestanding mountain in the world.

Adrenaline was high. Even with multiple layers, it seemed like the cold air was piercing through the body all the way to the bones. I think that's where the "bone-chilling cold" term might have originated. We immediately hit a steady ascending path, and the heart rate started to go up rapidly. Nose and throat felt dry, along with a burning sensation with every breath. Thanks to the water-spout from the hydration pack, I was sipping water frequently. After a few minutes, we settled into a slow but steady pace. It was a new experience to hike in the dark, with nothing but a few feet of light in front of me. The length of hiking poles had to be adjusted to account for the steep ascent. We had to lean forward all the time to maintain balance.

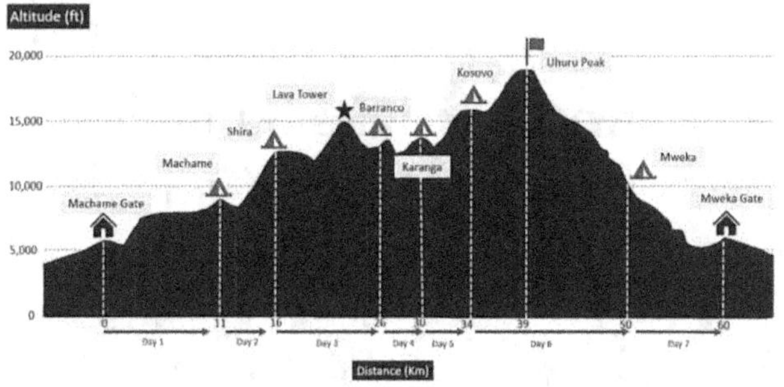

Kilimanjaro elevation profile

I was walking behind Owen. His footsteps were a useful reference for me to gauge the uneven trail. Breathing became heavier with each step. The warm, exhaled breath around the mouth was comforting, but soon I discovered an unforeseen issue. With my nose and mouth covered, heavy breathing was causing my eyeglasses to fog. Walking with the foggy glasses was risky; walking without them was equally problematic. I started sliding the balaclava away from my nose for a few seconds and then putting it back on to minimize the fogging.

Except for the guides checking in with us, no one said a word for the first hour. I think everyone was processing the shock of night-time hiking at the extremely high altitude. Nothing but rapid heartbeats and breathing to hear, head down, gaze focused near footsteps, vision limited just to the beam of the headlamp – it was a surreal walk through the dark. My steps settled into a rhythm - Right, Left, Right, Left, synchronized with silent chants of *"Paandurang Hari, Paandurang Hari*[8]*"*, and a rest-step after 10-15 steps.

We took a short break after a while. For the first time, I looked up in the direction of our ascent. I noticed tiny headlamps twinkling far away. A group of hikers had left before us and were making their way up the mountain. Back in the valley, I saw clusters of lights. Those were groups just beginning their ascent from their camps. Guessing from their position, it seemed like we were on a steep, almost 50-degree ascent! Who knows, I couldn't tell in the dark, but remembered reading about this stretch up to Stella Point, as one of the steepest and most demanding sections on the mountain. So here I was, tackling the most challenging section in pitch dark. Maybe it was a good thing, as I couldn't see the monumental challenge ahead of me or how far I still needed to go. Sometimes ignorance is a bliss. For now, all I had to

---

[8] One of the names of Lord Vishnu, commonly used in meditative chants

do was focus on my next step, put one foot in front of the other. Slow and steady was the name of the game.

We were now on a zigzag path - the endless switchbacks I had read about. The trail was becoming slippery with loose rocks and gravel. So far, we had relied on hiking poles to absorb and balance weight put on them during each step. Now, we had to be extra careful and ensure the poles didn't slip. Despite the balaclava, the uncovered part of my face was getting exposed to the bitter cold, making my eyes water often. Double trouble – foggy glasses and watery eyes! I had to stop every few minutes to clean my eyes and glasses. I tried climbing without eyeglasses for a while but started getting a headache.

After a couple of hours, we took another break. We cleared the path for passing hikers and sat on nearby rocks. I ate a snack bar and kept myself hydrated. Goodlove informed us that we were one-third of the way to the summit. For some, that was welcome news. For others, not so. They did not want to know how far we have come and how much was remaining. Goodlove had brought black tea and coffee in thermal containers. I opted for black tea. Getting hot liquid inside the body certainly felt good. It was a much-needed break. Feeling refreshed, I was ready to tackle the rest of the ascent. It was still dark, but I could notice a faint outline of the intimidating slope ahead. I didn't expect it to be easy, so just knowing that I was already one-third of the way was a significant morale boost.

One group of climbers passed us during the break. They, too, were breathing heavily. We marched on.

The black tea felt good for a while, but I soon felt that something was amiss. I dismissed any concern, thinking it may have been due to a combination of an odd time to drink tea, disrupted schedule, and cumulative exertion. Soon I started getting a stomach ache. Feeling uneasy, I slowed down. A few others in the group were also struggling to keep the pace.

Half an hour later, we took another short break. Hermant suggested that we form two groups - first at a regular pace, and second at a slightly slower pace. His estimation was both groups would reach the summit 20-30 minutes apart. I raised my hand for the second group. I thought I would be the only one, but after a few seconds, one by one, others raised their hands. Owen and Shannon wanted to get it over with quickly, so they decided to be in the first group. All others chose to be in the second group. Dev was getting a headache and started to feel dizzy. I told Hermant about my stomach pain and reflux issue. He advised me to take it slow and stay hydrated. Freddy led the first group. Hermant and Goodlove stayed with the second. It must have been around 4 am. While undertaking complex, lengthy tasks, I like breaking them down into manageable milestones. I turned my focus to the next milestone - seeing the sunrise from Stella Point. It was still about three hours away.

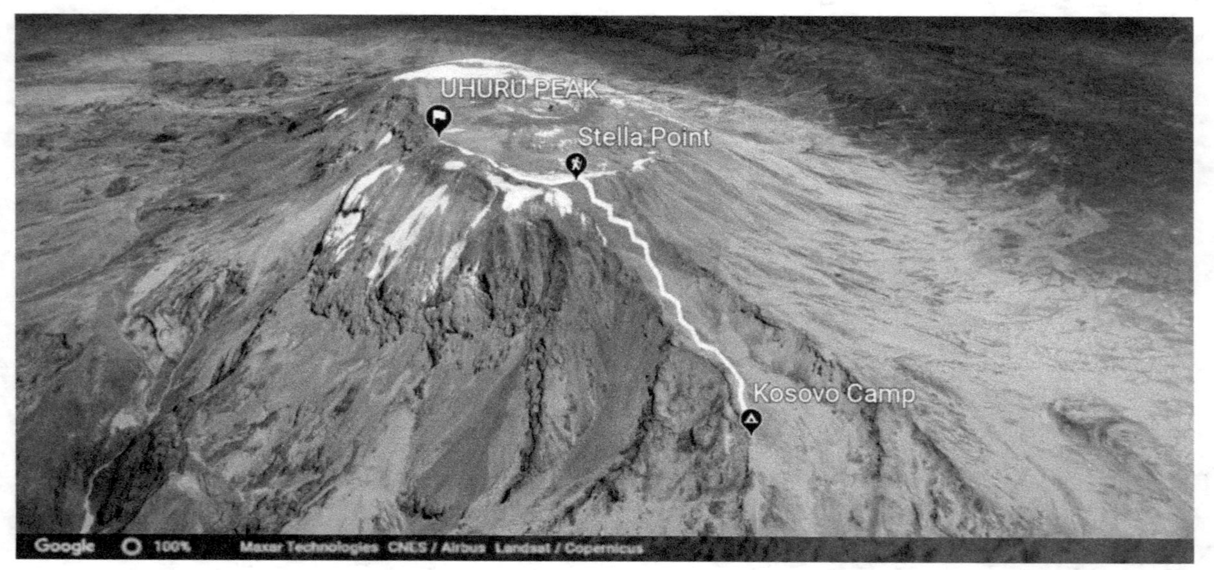

Summit ascent

I blocked every other thought out and kept marching forward. I realized that my hydration pack tube had frozen. It meant every time I wanted a sip of water - I had to stop, free my hands from hiking poles, rest the poles against my body, remove the water bottle from the side pocket, and then drink water. Compared to this, drinking from the hydration pack was so easy. Back to my rhythm - Right, Left, Right, Left.... *"Paandurang Hari, Paandurang Hari"*...

I wasn't feeling great after the tea-break. In a few minutes, I felt a painful reflux and had to stop by the side of the trail. I crouched down and threw up. It was a terrible feeling. My stomach felt squeezed, and everything inside was expelled. It was a worrying sign and a setback. After resting for a couple of minutes, I was ready to continue. I increased focus on my chants and rhythm, and soon caught up with my group. The slope had not let up even a bit.

Dev was walking in front of me and continued to struggle with dizziness. A couple of times, it seemed like he was losing balance. As a precaution, Goodlove started walking beside him. It seemed like all of us were walking like zombies. Hermant had a watchful eye on everyone and was checking in with me every few minutes. Another hour passed by. After throwing up once more, there was a noticeable drop in my energy level. I ate a snack bar from my backpack to replenish.

I was now desperately yearning for Stella Point. I had read that the worst part of the uphill climb would be over by that point. From there, it was an hour walk to the Uhuru Peak. At each opportunity, I looked up for signs of Stella Point. It seemed like time was running in slow motion. Physically almost drained, it was now time to summon my mental reserves.

"Think about the letters read last night...think about wishes from parents and siblings. Every word was full of love, support, and confidence in me. I have promised that I would conquer Kilimanjaro and come back home safely. I have always kept my promise to the family. I have never "not" done anything they wished and prayed for. Why would this be any different?"

The picture in my head was clear, a successful climb to the summit and back home safely. There was no other scenario. I reminded myself, the most crucial step is the next one, and kept pushing forward. At one break, I looked up and noticed our first group just a few feet ahead of us. After a dizzying hour, I finally saw the sky lighting up ever so slightly. It meant we should have been close to Stella Point. Hermant said we were still at least an hour away. Not what I wanted to hear at that point, but at least it gave me a reference.

Hermant and Goodlove kept checking in with each one of us frequently. Five climbers in the group, but no one had the energy to speak a word. We would just look at each other and communicate with a nod, a smile, or a thumbs-up. Weary faces, however, told the real story. Everyone had reached the limits of their physical ability and digging deep to continue.

Soon we passed a climber from another group who seemed to be in distress. Excruciating pain in the knees had forced him to turn back, just a couple of hours from the summit. I couldn't imagine the frustration of making such a difficult decision. I think he listened to his body, knew when to stop, and in the end, made the right decision.

We were now about 200 ft below Stella Point. In the faint pre-dawn light, it almost felt like a towering wall ahead of us. The switchbacks were now heavily covered with scree. You advance one step, and it slides back. That, coupled with a steep slope, made the last section towards Stella Point, the most challenging stretch on Kilimanjaro. Soon I noticed the sky lighting up. Realizing we wouldn't reach Stella Point in time for the sunrise, we decided to enjoy it from where we were.

It was an incomparable spot. Each climber sought out their own chosen place to experience the extraordinary moments. So far, a singular darkness had blanketed the earth and the sky. Soon, a distinct line formed separating the two, with a sliver of orange glow on the horizon. The sun signaled its arrival. A thick layer of white clouds had blanketed the valley. Slightly below the line of sight was Kili's second peak, Mawenzi. Gradually everything began to illuminate. I turned around and realized that an icefield surrounded me. Stalagmite-like ice structures covered surrounding rocks. The soft orange light reflecting from the white ice crystals was quite a sight to watch. The entire face of the mountain was glowing orange. The sun peeked from the horizon painting the sky in pastel colors. Soon the crimson sky changed to golden yellow. The Mawenzi peak transformed from a one-dimensional silhouette to a formidable mountain with its characteristic jagged top. It was one of the most magnificent sunrises I have ever witnessed!

Sunrise over Mawenzi

I still had to climb over 100 ft to reach Stella Point. After a herculean effort, we finally reached a big wooden signpost on a flat area welcoming us to the intermediate landmark. Stella Point (18,830 ft) is one of the three summit points on Kilimanjaro, next to Gilman's Point on the right and the actual summit - Uhuru Peak to the left. It is situated on top of the crater rim, which meant the worst part of the ascent, the heavy scree, was over. There was still over 500 ft climb to Uhuru Peak, but it would be mostly up and down on the crater rim at a relatively gentle gradient. But "relatively gentle" was of no comfort at that point. Some choose to end their climb at that point due to fatigue or altitude sickness. Climbers who reach that point get an official certificate from **KINAPA** for a successful attempt to Mount Kilimanjaro - with a minor difference, instead of Uhuru Peak, it says Stella

Point. It's a great achievement, nonetheless. The sense of satisfaction of reaching that point is immense.

Stella Point

I had read about the crater on Kibo being a magnificent sight in itself. It is named after Gustav Reusch, when he climbed the mountain for the twenty-fifth time out of sixty-five attempts during his lifetime. I walked a few feet north of the sign to see the natural wonder. The view was spectacular and gave a real sense of the depth and vastness of the crater. The crater bowl was nothing but a blackish inhospitable ash desert. It's a popular spot for geologists and die-hard mountaineers. With prior permits, some of these enthusiasts descend into the crater and camp overnight. That, of course, is very dangerous, given the likelihood of AMS at that altitude.

Hermant congratulated us and asked if anyone wanted to conclude the climb. No one was in the mood to stop there! We celebrated the achievement with a group picture before continuing to Uhuru Peak. We were about fifteen minutes behind our first group. It was a relatively gentle slope in the beginning, but things were becoming dire for me. After every 5-10 short steps, I had to rest. Hermant kept encouraging me.

"*Pole, Pole* Vikas. You are doing good. Take your time. We have less than an hour of this, and you will be at the peak. Can I carry your backpack, brother? It's okay. Most climbers give backpacks to their guides on the final day anyway. It will be easier for you."

"Asante Sana Hermant. I am okay to carry the backpack; there isn't much in it anyway."

I could see clusters of hikers lining the edge of the rim towards the Uhuru peak. Some were holding on to straps of their guide's backpacks for support and dragging themselves. A couple of hikers a few feet in front of me were painstakingly inching forward. I decided to use them as a reference and tried keeping pace with them. Everything was happening in super slow motion. Acid was still churning in my stomach. I removed my backpack, crouched down and rested for a couple of minutes before continuing.

I was now walking beside Rebmann Glacier. A thick mass of solid ice walls, the glacier is a small remnant of an enormous icecap which once crowned Kilimanjaro. The sun was shining on the glacier, making it a pristine world of glittering white. As breathtaking as it was, there was more to come. The ultimate tip of the peak, Uhuru, was still ahead.

Rebmann Glacier

As breathtaking as it was, there was more to come. The ultimate tip of the peak, Uhuru, was still ahead. This was the very last stretch. It was a contrasting set of circumstances - being extremely fatigued, and having a chance to see spectacular scenery, at the same time! As they say, the best view comes after the hardest climb. Hermant kept reminding me to enjoy the once-in-a-lifetime view, despite the fatigue. Walking beside the glacier on the left, vast expanse of the crater on the right, and tantalizingly close Uhuru Peak straight ahead, was a surreal experience. I had to dig deep for strength. There was a constant voice in my head,

"Don't quit. Finish what you have started. Failure is not an option. I must push through this final wall. How do champions do it? Think about Roger Federer - 2017 Australian Open Championship, down 1-3 in the fifth set against arch-nemesis Nadal.

Federer found a way to score an emphatic win. What can you learn from that? Focus, dig deep, turn the tide. Think about Sachin Tendulkar's 1998 Desert Storm[9] – back to back knocks against Australia. Can you beat your best? Fight for glory, fight until you have nothing left, fight to the finish..."

The thoughts propelled me forward. After another half an hour, I could see the Uhuru Peak signpost! With nothing in my stomach to fuel me, the last 2.5-3 km walk on the crater rim was the most treacherous walk of my life! It took me one and a half hours to cover the distance between Stella Point to Uhuru Peak. On a regular mountain, it would have taken me less than thirty minutes, but this was no ordinary mountain, and nothing about the 19,000 ft elevation was normal!

____

[9] Cricket legend Sachin Tendulkar's world-famous batting inning against Australia in 1998 semi-final played in Sharjah, where temperatures reached 41° Celsius and play was halted for 25 minutes due to a wild sandstorm. The innings swept Australia off its feet, establishing Sachin as the best batsman in contemporary cricket. He backed up his talent with another memorable knock in the finals to win the tournament for India.

Final stretch to the Uhuru peak

Adrenaline took over, and I pushed myself towards the sign. It was a rush, and finally, around 9 am I was at the Uhuru Peak! I made it! I made it!! I actually made it!!! A euphoric feeling of happiness, relief, and accomplishment washed over me. The surge of emotions was overwhelming. Since last night I had blocked them to focus on the task in hand. I collapsed on my knees, and tears started rolling down. Nothing was holding them back now. With my face covered in my palms, I let it all go. Yes, I did keep my promise! After the outlet of emotions, I bowed down to mother nature for helping me set foot on the peak.

All my fellow climbers in the second group had reached before me. Shannon and Owen from the first group were already on their way back. Everyone made it! Congratulations, cheers, and smiles all around. Fatigue was forgotten, and once again, adrenaline ruled the moment. We took pictures to commemorate the special occasion. Then I pulled out papers with pictures of deities and family from my pocket. Everyone was curious, so I told them about what they meant to me. Then from the other side pocket, I took out the Indian flag and Shivaji Maharaj's *Bhagava* flag. All symbols of honor. I took pictures with all of them with Uhuru Peak's plank in the background. It was a proud moment. Hermant was impressed to see the family bond I had. Being a family man himself, he started calling me "Family Boy". Freddy and Goodlove endorsed his choice. It was a nickname I gladly accepted.

After the celebrations, we all just sat there, admiring the beauty and soaking in the grandeur of the serene view. The sun was shining, and the sky was crystal blue with no trace of clouds. The temperature was almost comfortable, and the visibility unlimited. I was indeed on the roof of Africa! The view was even more impressive than I imagined. I went to the side and recorded a message for my family, capturing the panoramic view from the summit.

Proud moment!

After about twenty minutes, Hermant and Freddy "encouraged" us to head back down. It was tempting to spend more time there, for which we had toiled relentlessly for six days, but the thin air and the altitude made it dangerous. In the past expeditions, people spending more time at the summit had passed out due to exhaustion and lack of oxygen. We began the return journey with a renewed spring in the step. Admiring the incredible views of the glacier and crater, once again, we soon reached the Stella Point.

The mission was not complete yet. As the saying goes – going to the top is optional, coming back is mandatory. With a bright and sunny morning upon us, I had a bird's eye view of the insane distance and steep mountain-face we had climbed up in the dark. We now had to climb that down. It would be the ultimate test of endurance and a grueling challenge for the knees. With the adrenaline rush over, climbing down was a mighty struggle. I had slowed down considerably, so Hermant asked the rest of the group to go ahead with Goodlove. I kept moving one step at a time. I reached Kosovo camp at around 1 pm, an hour later than the rest of the group. The group was aware of my struggles after the unfortunate tea-break, and some didn't think I would make it to the top. They had just finished lunch in the dining tent, and when they saw me come down on my own feet, everyone clapped and congratulated me! Their support and appreciation meant a lot to me.

I suspected that I got hit with the stomach flu. Worrying that it may be contagious, I called Dev, the pharmacist, outside the tent, and described my symptoms. To get relief from the acid reflux, he advised taking antacids and gave me a few tablets. I tried eating some rice and soup and went back to my tent for rest. We had to leave soon for the Mweka camp.

Hermant came to my tent to check up on me. There was still 7-8 km of a downhill hike remaining. With some food and fluid in my stomach, I was hoping to have enough energy and decided to tough it out. It was again time to revitalize myself. That's one great thing about conquering seemingly insurmountable challenges - next time you face them, you can count on the strength and experience gained from previous ones. Fresh from the triumph, I cheered myself and got ready for the next phase.

I stayed with the group for the first couple of hours, but my troubles were not over yet. I started having diarrhea. Sensing my problems, Hermant asked the rest of the group to go ahead. Shannon was fatigued and had slowed down. For the next hour, it was Shannon and me under Hermant's watchful eye, inching our way towards Mweka camp.

To make matters worse, a couple of showers rolled by, and fog started to limit visibility. Hermant called some porters on his walkie talkie. He asked Shannon to go with one of them, and others to stay back with him. I didn't understand why he called for additional help. After an hour and a couple of bathroom breaks later, I noticed the trail disappearing into a dried rocky stream. I wasn't sure if I was hallucinating or if the cascade of rocks was real! Hermant confirmed my fear and cautioned that the trail going forward would be difficult. His call for additional help now started to make sense.

There had been many accidents on that stretch with tired hikers slipping, falling, or rolling their ankles, sustaining severe injuries. At several points, I had to use both hands and feet to scramble down - many places where the next foothold was 5-6 ft deep. Even on a regular day, it was a challenging descent. Each step was becoming dangerous for me. Two porters started walking beside me to ensure I didn't lose footing.

Gradually light faded, and we were scrambling in the dark with the help of headlamps. A few more porters joined us, many of them not even part of our mountain crew. Hermant commanded such respect with local climbing agencies that when other groups at Mweka Camp heard that he called for help, they voluntarily joined us. I was overwhelmed with their support. It was a special brotherhood! Everyone rallied and helped me get through the never-ending cascade of rocks. Throughout the ordeal, instinctively, I was chanting *"Paandurang Hari, Paandurang Hari"* at each step. Later Hermant told me that even the porters had learned the chant and repeated it with me. The entire group was cheerful, funny, and kept me engaged in talks. I wouldn't have come out of that stretch safely without their support. It was pitch dark when I reached Mweka Camp at around 8 pm. Just unreal that I climbed down almost half of Kilimanjaro in that situation.

Everyone had finished dinner and retired to their tents. Hermant gave me hot water to freshen up and helped set up my sleeping bag. Freddy brought a dinner plate with rice and some fruits in it. Despite trying hard, I couldn't eat anything. Descending to a lower altitude was not showing any improvements in my symptoms, so they didn't think my sickness was altitude related. After some discussion, they gave me anti-diarrhea tablets. I didn't have any words to describe the gratitude I felt towards their kind gestures. It was another cold night, but after an extremely eventful and intense twenty-hour stretch of my life, I was ready to sleep.

* * *

12. Mweka Camp to Mweka Gate

Climb Day 7 - October 2, 2018

I woke up at 7 am to the sounds around my tent. Last day! Final 4,500 ft and 10 km to go. The finish line was in sight. I was surprised that there was no wake-up call. Still feeling drained, I just stayed in my sleeping bag for a while. I was about to step out of the tent when Hermant came by.

"Jambo Vikas. How are you feeling?"

"Good morning. Just tired and weak. So here we are, final day. I will get ready soon."

"Okay. Take your time. I will ask others to leave soon with Freddy and Goodlove. When you are ready, I will accompany you to the Mweka Gate."

"Hermant, thanks a lot for everything you and the rest of the crew did last night. Really grateful for your help. I would like to give something to the crew members as a token of appreciation. Something that will be helpful to them. Any thoughts?"

"You don't have to! It's part of our job and who we are. All of us enjoyed having you on this trip. Last night you helped yourself, we were just giving you company."

"Asante Sana Hermant, but you have to tell me what would help the crew?"

"Nothing comes to my mind. They will be thrilled to see you in good health, that's it."

Not getting any ideas from Hermant, I had to come up with something useful. I thought, given their daily grind on the mountain, the porters would benefit from having extra warm gear. I opened my bag and removed all the warm clothes, socks, gloves, winter cap, snacks, moisturizer, hand sanitizers - anything that would be useful to them - and packed it in a plastic bag. I also prepared an envelope with customary tips plus some extra amount for the entire crew. I had regular shoes and decided to give my hiking boots to the porters.

After getting ready, I gave the bag and envelope to Hermant. Every climber gave customary tips for the porters on the last day, but the extra bag was unexpected. Hermant was pleasantly surprised. With gratitude on his face, he shook my hands and said,

"Asante Sana! That's really nice of you to think about the crew. I would just ask you to take the hiking boots back. You have been through a lot on this expedition. Any hiker should keep their expedition boots as a memory of the adventure."

His suggestion made sense, and I decided to keep the hiking boots. It was satisfying to see the happiness on his face. He was a proud man, a man with honor. Even if he needed something for the crew, I don't think he would have asked me or any of his clients.

I managed to eat some rice, took another dose of anti-diarrhea tablet, and got ready for the last stretch. Now, we had a logistics and time challenge. The bus carrying us from the Mweka gate to the hotel had to leave by 1 pm. It was about a two-three hour ride to the hotel, including a lunch break. I had to leave the hotel by 5 pm to catch my flight back home. The airport was another hour drive from the hotel. Given all these dependencies, there was not much time in the schedule to accommodate my slow pace. Reaching the Mweka gate later than 1 pm was not an option. Which meant I had about 4 hours to descend 4,500 ft over 10 km! Given my frail condition, I would have needed at least six-eight hours. Time was not on my side.

Hermant had talked to the park authorities and had arranged a one-wheeled stretcher to carry me. There were two options - I could walk like yesterday, which most likely would take longer, or let the porters carry me on the stretcher, which would be quicker.

Time constraints didn't leave me much choice. The porters strapped me and my bag on the stretcher, and we left at 8:30 am.

It's not how I wanted to finish my last day on Kili. We were in a forest zone now, similar to the first day. Initially, the trail was level, and the porters were fast. Within ten minutes, we passed my group. Soon the trail became uneven, making the ride quite bumpy. Despite the porter's best efforts, my head started to hurt with the constant banging. I couldn't take it anymore.

"Hermant, let's take a break. The porters are doing great, but the ride doesn't seem a good idea. You have given me a head start now. Can I try walking on my own? If I fall behind, I will get on the stretcher again."

We agreed to give it a try. With Hermant and his cheerful crew for the company, I started walking. The trail was not as steep or dangerous as yesterday. As much as time allowed, I preferred to walk than endure the head-banging ride. I gave it all, and then some, to finally reach the Mweka Gate. It's amazing how adrenaline and euphoria mask unbearable pain!

The entire crew cheered. I gave each one of them a big hug. The rest of the group soon reached Mweka gate. We all congratulated each other and took final group pictures at a sign declaring completion of the Kilimanjaro expedition. After seven days, we were seeing the first signs of civilization - people, buildings, and toilets. Yes, toilets - real clean toilets with running water. Treating running water as a novelty, we freshened up to our heart's content! One final time, we lined up outside the Mweka registration hut and entered our names in the KINAPA register.

The bus came on time. I sat in a window seat with a gentle breeze flowing over my face. Oh, the simple pleasures of life! With a whirlwind of thoughts in my mind, I dozed off. About an hour later, we stopped at a hotel for a celebration lunch. It was a nice hotel with an artistic ambiance, and the food seemed good. I was still drained. I knew I had to get solid food in my stomach, but I didn't feel like eating anything. Reluctantly, I gave it a try and managed to eat some plain rice. My biggest relief was that everything I ate in the morning had stayed in my stomach. There was a souvenir shop beside the hotel. Luckily, because of the quick lunch, I had about ten minutes to shop. I remembered that I still had to buy the "I Climbed Kili" t-shirt. With a stroke of luck, the shop had that exact piece. Now that I had truly earned the tag, I bought that t-shirt and a few other souvenirs for my family.

Everyone quickly boarded the bus. A guest performer joined us for the remaining journey. He sang in Swahili and played catchy tunes on the guitar. The porters started cheering and singing. All of us began clapping to his songs. Even though we were dead-tired, it brought smiles on our faces. It made the ride more entertaining.

One by one, the porters started to get down at their destination. It was emotional to say good-bye to them. These were the good Samaritans who worked tirelessly behind the scene to make the climb a success. A few more songs and drop-offs later, the bus reached the hotel. We again gathered in the lobby, one last time, where Hermant distributed the official Kilimanjaro certificates. A piece of paper never felt so precious! Saying goodbye to him was difficult.

"Thank you, brother! You are a remarkable human being and a true leader. I couldn't have done this trek without you and your amazing crew. I don't have words to express my gratitude."

"Don't say anything! You did extremely well despite being sick. It was a pleasure taking you on the mountain. You are like a brother from another mother! Take care of yourself and the family. Have a safe trip back home. Tell your parents they have raised a good kid."

With a hug, a handshake, and tears in eyes, we said goodbye to each other.

I had less than an hour to get ready for the airport. The front desk called for a taxi and asked me to be prepared in the lobby by 5:30 pm. My room was on the far corner of the third floor. There was no elevator. The last thing I wanted to do was climb up the stairs and walk! I didn't have the time or energy to talk to the hotel staff for a different room.

Back in the room, I arranged my bags, wrapped dirty clothes from the last seven days in a couple of plastic bags before packing them in my suitcase. Now to a much-missed luxury - a hot shower! It's hard to explain the pleasure of taking a hot shower after seven days out in the cold wilderness. I was enjoying every second of it, but in a few minutes, the water ran cold. The water geyser in the bathroom was small, and I had already used up the hot water. I had to either take a cold shower or wait for the water to get warm. Like other slip-ups in this hotel, I decided to shrug it off and move on. At 5 pm, there was a knock on my door. The hotel staff told me that the taxi driver was waiting. I wasn't expecting him for another thirty minutes, but I got ready and rushed to the taxi.

On the way to the airport, I called my family and shared the news of the successful expedition first-hand. They were getting daily email updates from the climbing agency and occasional texts from me. Still, hearing my voice made it more real for them. There was a sense of relief and satisfaction now that the expedition was complete. I bid farewell to the scenic towns of Moshi and Arusha, and made it to the airport just in time for the flight.

The flight back to the USA felt very long, as I couldn't wait to see my family. My mind was still replaying various events from the last seven days. So many times, I just woke up from my sleep startled, thinking I was still on the mountain with a long distance to cover.

* * *

13. Home Sweet Home

Varsha, Titiksha, and Tanishtha came to the airport for pick-up. It was a great feeling to see and hug them. Back home, they had decorated the house - balloons, cards, and best of all, a photo-cake with my picture from Machame Gate! We spent the next few days talking about the adventure, the incredible people I met, and the otherworldly sites I witnessed. It was good to be back home. Physical recovery took a few more days. I think more than the stories and pictures, my daughters were happy, and my wife was relieved that I was back home with them- home sweet home!

While in Kili, having the return flight on the last day of the expedition didn't sound like a good idea to some in my group. For me, it was different. After completing the adventure of my life, I wanted to be with my family as soon as possible. Being anywhere else would have been very uncomfortable. For some time on the last day, it didn't seem like a wise decision, but in the end, it turned out the way I imagined.

After a few weeks, I went to India to visit my parents, siblings, and the rest of the family. There too, the celebration was memorable! The house was decorated with my Kilimanjaro pictures. My parents, brother, sister, nephew, nieces - all gathered, and I talked about highs and lows on the mountain. Everyone was happy and proud of the achievement. Meeting my parents was when I truly felt the adventure was over and was well worth it. There is no bigger joy for me than making my family proud, especially my parents. Now I could say with pride - Mission Accomplished!

Celebrations with wife and daughters

Family. Inspiration. Everything.

* * *

14. Concluding Thoughts

I am often asked - "Was it worth climbing Kilimanjaro?" "Would you advise others to do it?" My answer to the first question is always *Yes*— a big, emphatic *Yes!* And the answer to the second question is - Yes, but with some caveats.

Kili is an extraordinary adventure, an almost sublime experience. It is exhausting. It is hardship, no doubt about it. During the summit ascent and return to Mweka, I pushed through walls, walls I didn't even realize were there. Yet the real revelation is that it's possible to get to that sublime moment, by putting just one foot in front of the other. For most people, it will be the most challenging climb, physically and mentally, they will ever do. To decide whether to take on an adventure like Kilimanjaro, you need to start with the "Why?" There must be a very good reason to put yourself through that ordeal. You can just do it for the thrill of it, but I believe the satisfaction is much greater if the reason is larger than yourself. It will always stay with you. You can continue to draw strength from it. It has the power to fuel further life-changing outcomes and inspire people around you. The result, whether you climb Kilimanjaro for a good reason or no reason, is the same - you conquered the tallest free-standing mountain in the world. But the impact of that result, if you have the right rationale, is far-reaching and much more valuable. I believe humans are capable of having a more profound and meaningful purpose.

On Kilimanjaro, I met several climbers with varying degrees of background and ability. Some of them had climbed the mountain several times. Their stories were awe-inspiring. A couple of them just struck me as oddballs, though. Although experts in mountaineering, they seemed to have no respect for the mountain, and their reasons for climbing were very shallow. Most of it was about themselves, to have the bragging rights, to show-off, and to somehow elevate their standing in the society. To me, such goals are narrow-minded. These individuals lacked respect for the local people and their culture, frequently using derogatory terms to describe them and the mountain. That's one thing I could never understand. The mountain has been there for eons, it doesn't ask anyone to climb it, and is revered by locals as a sacred place. It provides livelihood to thousands of people and natural habitat to thousands of species. Instead of showing nothing but respect, instead of being grateful to have an opportunity to climb it, instead of being in awe of the spectacular beauty, why would anyone disrespect the breathtaking wonder? It makes no sense and reminds me of lines from the show "Altered Carbon" that I watched recently - "Humanity is spread to the stars, but no matter how far we venture into the unknown, the worst monsters are those we bring with us..."

Before embarking on Kilimanjaro's arduous adventure, I had written down my reasons. It all boiled down to:

1. Make my family proud.
2. Set an example of how to overcome adversity with hard work and perseverance.
3. Take control of health, Test endurance and mental resolve.
4. Experience the unbridled glory of African wildlife and Mt. Kilimanjaro.
5. Be the best version of myself.

It was quite an epic journey that taught me a lot about the power of visualization, conditioning mind, knowing yourself, and setting expectations.

Power of visualization:

Throughout my preparation, I used to visualize each day on Kili, each activity from morning to bedtime. I would rerun the loop to anticipate challenges I might face, things I may need, and things I could do better. It was as important as the physical training. I dreamt of so many scenarios on the mountain. Still, one scenario never crossed my mind - me not making the summit. No matter the difficulties, I always saw myself reaching the Uhuru peak. In the last couple of days on Kilimanjaro, when the situation was dire, it was this power of visualization and dogged determination that pushed me across the finish line.

Conditioning the mind:

On any arduous mountain journey, some moments reinforce your belief that you're going to get through it successfully. The first such moment for me was the morning of the third day, when I realized that my body handled two rigorous days at high altitude without much trouble. The second one was when I conquered the Barranco wall with relative ease. The third and the most critical moment was after dinner the night before the summit. After five long days of hiking, we all had reached our limits. But one small trick to condition my mind did wonders. It was about "resetting" the mind back to the beginning. I knew it was impossible to "forget" the beating my body took in the previous five days. But mentally, it was critical to erase the past and focus on the next day with renewed energy. The final ascent was all mental. As Frank Sonnenberg says, - *"Ability determines if you can; attitude determines if you will."* Having the right attitude and a reconditioned mind, focused on what's ahead, really made a big difference. In life, too, conditioning your mind - especially when faced with adversity - can do wonders.

Knowing Yourself and Setting Expectations:

I don't consider myself a very fit person. At best, my fitness level is average. I know my limitations, but I am also aware of my strengths and areas where I can push myself further. What I may lack in fitness, I compensate with unwavering passion and will-power. I always believed in having a clear understanding of things I can control and things I cannot. Training as hard as I can for Kilimanjaro was in my control. How my body reacts to extreme temperature and altitude was not in my control. It was unknown. But the unknown did not deter me from focusing on things I could do. I expected the climb to be rigorous, to be exhausting, to push me to the brink of my physical limits. I expected the final push to be mostly a mental battle. I expected I would have to dig deep to find the inner strength and the resolve that comes from the courage of conviction. Conviction in my reason, in my preparation, and in love and wishes from my family. Having expected a tough road ahead, I was able to prepare well and be ready to react with poise to any unknowns. Being self-aware and managing expectations played a big part in my success.

Life is a book full of adventures. Kilimanjaro is a memorable chapter in the book of my life. An unforgettable journey that taught me a lot about myself and the world around me. I am forever grateful to everyone who made this adventure possible!

* * *

References

For the preparation of Kilimanjaro trek and Safari, and for writing this book, I have found the following resources quite helpful.

- Kilimanjaro - The Trekking Guide to Africa's Highest Mountain: All-in-one guide for climbing Kilimanjaro – by Henry Stedman
- www.machame.com
- www.ultimatekilimanjaro.com

www.ingramcontent.com/pod-product-compliance
Lightning Source LLC
Chambersburg PA
CBHW070805240726

48654CB00007B/215